DIRECTION IN PRAYER

DIRECTION IN PRAYER

Studies in Ascetic Method

EDITED BY
PATRICK THOMPSON
FOR THE SOCIETY OF
RETREAT CONDUCTORS

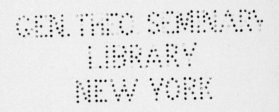
LONDON
SOCIETY FOR PROMOTING
CHRISTIAN KNOWLEDGE
NORTHUMBERLAND AVENUE, W.C. 2

First Published in 1933

PRINTED IN GREAT BRITAIN

CONTENTS

PART II

SOME METHODS OF PRAYER

PART III

DIRECTION IN PRAYER

APPENDIX

INTRODUCTION

THE publication of these studies was first undertaken in the hope that they might lead others, besides those for whom they were originally written, to realise that there is need of serious and continued study if we are to assimilate and make use of the stores of wisdom which the experience of past ages in the Church has bequeathed to us. The obligation of such study is, of course, in the first place, incumbent upon priests. For upon them is laid the weighty responsibility of "writing in souls," of teaching others how to hold themselves open to the visits of Him whose "delights are to be with the sons of men." This they can scarcely hope to do unless they have themselves tasted the sweets of this divine friendship, which is the heart of all religion.

Others besides priests, however, learners as well as teachers, devout laity no less than religious, may be willing to welcome such help as this book can give them in the acquisition of the science of the saints. For, though prayer is, as the first chapter strives to show, a "natural," that is to say a reasonable, attitude for man in view of his supernatural destiny, that does not mean that it is easy. For fallen man to establish and maintain himself in communion with God, it is not enough to fold his hands and close his eyes, nor even to go down upon his knees. For prayer, it is contended, is an attitude of the whole being; and there are large tracts of man's being to which, in his present state, such an attitude is highly uncongenial.

The first chapter, then, attempts to demonstrate that such an attitude is exacted by man's very constitution as a creature, conscious of his creaturehood. The next recalls the proclamation of this fact by the Son of God, the Incarnate Word, who was, as Bérulle called Him, *le religieux du Père* ; and proceeds to sketch the development of the interpretation of the divine precept of prayer, enunciated and exemplified by Christ, among His followers in the Church, the worshipping body, down the ages.

The third chapter sums up the results of the reflection of these ages on the nature of the road travelled by all who have tried to live the life of prayer, and enumerates the stages which have been distinguished on this road. The practical use to which such distinctions are to be put emerges later, in the final chapters on Direction.

The second section of the book comprises four chapters on the great historical methods of mental prayer. S. Ignatius Loyola, by the methods which he originated, first brought systematic mental prayer out of the cloister, and S. Francis de Sales, working upon his materials, firmly established it in the world, where, hitherto, a more or less intelligent participation in the liturgy and its derivatives had been the staple of the prayer-life of devout layfolk. Second only in importance to the Jesuit and Salesian spirituality which made its direct impact upon the laity in the sixteenth and seventeenth centuries, and still inspires a wider field of Christian devotion than any other system, comes " the French School " of the Oratory, S. Sulpice, the Eudists, and the many movements connected with the name of S. Vincent de Paul. This school should have a special interest for us to-day, in view of its chosen method of working from the centre outwards, and attacking, in the first place, the problem of the reform of the clergy.

The " Way of Renewal," for example, loses something of its novelty in the light of the *Conférences de Mardi*— one of the forces which went to make a Bossuet. This French school had a wider influence than is sometimes realised (not, alas! always uncontaminated by traces of that Jansenism which was its bane) upon our own revival of the last century; and its leaders were scarcely behind the Jesuits in their efforts to spread the use of that most searching instrument of spiritual regeneration, the retreat.

From this review of methods and systems we pass, in the third section of the book, to the problem of problems —their application to the individual soul. Here the great lesson, enforced by a catena of quotations from all the great masters of the art of arts, is the necessity for self-effacement on the part of the director. One after another these masters urge upon him the duty of subordinating, not only his private whims and fancies, but also the methods and systems which they have themselves elaborated from their experience of direc-tion, to the evident leadings of the Holy Spirit in the soul under direction, at whatever stage of development it may be.

But this is not to deny that the director needs the science of his art, or that reading must supplement experience in giving it to him. The director's touch must be light, but it must also be sure, and he must be equipped with the knowledge which will enable him to recognise the symptoms of a soul's state when he meets them, as he must, for the first time. For though the great principles to be inculcated in direction—recollec-tion, mortification, humility—are the same at all stages of progress, the ways in which they are effectively to be applied vary with all the gradations through which a soul can pass from the first infusion of faith to the final establishment in union with the Divine. This, the most important section of the book, will not have failed of its purpose if it succeeds in persuading one priest, or aspirant to the priesthood, that good intentions and common-sense are insufficient equipment for the delicate work of directing souls in prayer.

In an appendix to the book will be found some notes on teaching children to pray.

PART I

THE THEORY OF PRAYER

I. THE DOGMATIC BASIS

By HERBERT MATHER

1. *The Necessity of Prayer*

WE shall have small hope of learning *how* to pray unless we are first clearly convinced of *why* we must pray. We must, then, recall and emphasise these three foundation truths; that prayer is a *duty*; that it is a *privilege*; and that it is pre-eminently the *duty* and the *privilege* of *priests*. Prayer is a *duty*; it springs out of the fundamental relationship of man to his Creator. That relationship is one of dependence; therefore it must be expressed in *abasement* before the *mysterium tremendum*. Prayer is a *privilege*; man is a creature, but a creature made to the image of God; an intelligent creature of an intelligible God; therefore the relationship of man to God must also take the form of *aspiration* towards the *mysterium fascinans*. Prayer is the recognition of a God at once transcendent and immanent.

The historical sequence of Grace, Sin, Revelation and Redemption only goes to emphasise and underline these eternal truths, and to make prayer Christian prayer; a response to a God who has deigned to make plain our duty, and who condescends to share our privilege, who will teach us to pray, and become man in order to pray with us. And in these sublime functions the Christian priest is admitted to participate.

S. Thomas à Kempis, in the *Imitation of Christ*, tells us: " I had rather feel compunction than know how to define it." This is his emphatic way of teaching us

7

that the following of Christ is a matter more of the
heart than of the head. Life, in the sense of the
Scholastics, was essentially motion arising within a soul
and coming to rest outside its starting-point. Here
below, then, Christian life was action, rather than
contemplation; warfare, rather than peace.

And if, at times, we turn back upon our own action,
and reflect upon what we do when we pray, it is not
so much in order that we may acquire a merely theo-
retical knowledge, but rather that we may learn to
pray better ourselves and, as a result, be better able
to help others to pray.

The first question which the mind is driven to ask
itself when it thus reflects upon its own action in prayer
is: "Why do I pray?" And our answer to this question will be conditioned by the notion we have framed
of what prayer is: if prayer is petition and nothing
more, then we pray in order to get something. Our
first task, then, must be to improve upon this very
inadequate notion of what prayer is, or is meant to be.

In S. Paul's analysis of the function of reason in the
province of faith, which he addressed to the Christians
at Rome, there is a striking passage which points to the
necessity of prayer: "For the invisible things of him
from the creation of the world are clearly seen, being
understood by the things that are made, even his
eternal power and Godhead; so that they are without excuse." [1] S. Thomas Aquinas, in his commentary
on this passage, tells us: "But these three points refer
to the three ways of knowing God. For the invisible
things of God are known by way of negation, His eternal
power by way of causality, and His divinity by way of
super-excellence." Walter Hilton dilates upon this
same theme, as follows: "Holy Writ saith, that a soul

[1] Rom. i. 20.

that will find God must lift her inward eye upward, and seek God above itself. Then some men that would do after this saying, understand this word 'above themselves' to signify the placing or setting of a thing in place and worthiness above another, as one element or planet is above another in situation and worthiness of a bodily place. But it is not so taken spiritually; for a soul is above each bodily thing, not in place, or sight, but in purity and worthiness of nature. Right so in the same manner God is above all bodily and spiritual creatures, not in place and sight, but in purity and worthiness of His unchangeable blessed nature. And therefore he that will wisely seek God, and find Him, he must not run out with his thoughts as if he would climb above the sun, and part the firmament, and imagine the Majesty like to a hundred suns. But he must rather draw down the sun, and all the firmament, and forget it, and cast it beneath him where he is, and set all this and all bodily things also at nought; and then, if he can, think spiritually both of himself and of God also. And if he do thus, then seeth the soul above itself, then seeth it into heaven. Upon this same manner shall this word 'within' be understood. It is commonly said that a soul should see our Lord within all things and within itself. True it is, that our Lord is within all creatures, but not on that manner that a kernel is hid within the shell of a nut; or as a little bodily thing is contained within a greater. But He is within all creatures, as holding and preserving them in their being, through the subtlety and power of His own blessed nature, and purity invisible. For even as a thing that is most precious and most clean is laid innermost, right so by the same likeness it is said that the nature of God, which is most precious, most clean, most goodly, most remote from bodily substance, is hid within all things. And therefore he that will seek God within, he must first forget all bodily things, for all such things are without; and also his own body; and he must forget thinking of his own soul, and think on the uncreated nature; that is, Jesus (sic), who made him, and giveth him reason, memory and love, the which is within him through His power and sovereign subtlety." [1]

If these are true ideas of God, then we, His creatures, are meant to enter into the closest relationship with Him, and as a result have very definite duties towards Him. Between person and person the virtue that gives each his due is justice. The virtue whereby man gives God His due, or, to use the more familiar phrase, does his duty to God, is religion. The first of these duties is to acknowledge that it was God who made us. Thus we can say that prayer is an act of the virtue of religion whereby we acknowledge that God is the Maker and Mover of all things, without any of the imperfections that exist in created things, and Himself infinitely perfect in being. When we recognise that our Maker has every possible perfection, then we may be said to recognise that God is above us. *Every effort of ours to recognise this is prayer.* The simple definition of S. John Damascene, that prayer is the uplifting of the mind to God, covers every God-ward movement of the soul, from the half-formed longing to believe to the never-ceasing alleluias of the saints in heaven. Dr. Liddon says much the same when he defines prayer as: " The act by which man, conscious at once of his weakness and of his immortality, puts himself into real and effective communication with the almighty, the eternal, the self-existent God." [2]   Whenever the soul of man engages in

<hr />

[1] Walter Hilton, *Scale of Perfection*, pp. 242-3.
[2] H. P. Liddon, *Some Elements of Religion*, p. 166.

prayer it must rely on its belief in the existence of a great bond between itself and God.

Thus prayer includes the whole cycle of possible communication between the soul and God; it implies the whole spiritual action of the soul turned towards God as its true end and adequate object. "Minds religiously affected," says Hooker, " are wont, in everything of weight and moment which they do or see, to examine according unto the riches of piety what dependency it hath of God, what reference to themselves, what coherence with any of these duties whereunto all things in the world should lead, and accordingly they frame the inward disposition of their minds to admire God, sometimes to bless Him and give Him thanks, sometimes to exult in His love, sometimes to implore His mercy. All which different elevations of spirit unto God are contained in the name of prayer." [1] It is essential on every practical ground to recollect this wider meaning of prayer. For if in our habitual thoughts we narrow it down to petition, it becomes entirely self-centred.

2. *The Value of Prayer*

If prayer, then, is really an endeavour to conform our whole being to the will of God, based on the yearning of the image towards its prototype, of like towards like, then the study of its nature will at once reveal its necessity and emphasise its serious importance as a response to the divine intention. The ancient and universal natural instinct to pray is nothing less in reality than His voice moving us to Himself who is the Author of the nature in which this instinct is implanted. Alike in nature and in grace there is the necessity for a frank and full recognition of the primary law of

[1] Hooker, *Ecclesiastical Polity*, V. xlviii. 2.

B

dependence on God which is the basis of all religion. To priests this may seem self-evident, but priests, and indeed all Christians who have to teach at all, realise that the majority of people to-day do not believe it. And therefore, if they would teach others to pray, they must start from the foundation principle of S. Ignatius, that man depends on God.

Prayer has been called the breath of the soul, which points to the fact that, as the body cannot live without breathing, so a soul without prayer is dead. Man must keep in touch with God if he is to fulfil the purpose for which he is made; he can neither praise, reverence, nor serve God without prayer. Prayer is essential to the harmonious development of our whole being. And because God is the Father who loves us, He has not left us to find this fact out for ourselves, but has Himself commanded us " to pray always and not to faint " (Luke xviii. 1). The profound human instinct to pray has been sanctioned and enforced by commands which fell from the lips of the Son of God Himself. As a consequence of His teaching, the Apostles represent prayer as not so much one activity of the Christian life among others, as its instinctive and characteristic movement.

This, of course, is not to deny that petition is a part, and a great part, of all Christian prayer. But we must remember that it is not necessary for us to set forth our petitions before God in order to make known to Him our minds and desires, but rather in order that we ourselves may realise that in all things we must have recourse to the divine assistance, and thus learn more fully our dependence on God and our need of His help. We do not aim at changing the divine arrangements, but at obtaining by our prayers what God has arranged to give us. God, indeed, bestows on us many things out of His generosity, even things for which we do not ask; but He wishes to grant us some things on the condition that we ask for them. And this is for our advantage, for it is intended to give us confidence in having recourse to God, as well as to make us realise that He is the Author of all good in us. Hence S. Chrysostom says: " Reflect what great happiness is bestowed on you, what glory is given you—namely, to converse in your prayers with God, to join in colloquy with Christ, and to beg for what you wish or desire." [1]

And elsewhere: [2] " Prayer, then, is not necessary on God's account, as though He needed to be informed of our wants, or could not be happy without our homage, or might be induced to change His plans; it is necessary for our own sakes, for, although God could and sometimes does grant favours unasked, He wishes that ordinarily we should have the double benefit of the prayer and of the favour given in answer to the prayer." God could grant the crops of the field without human cultivation, or even tools and finished articles without human invention or labour, but man would then lose the fruits that belong to labour of mind and body. Prayer is most beneficial, even when unanswered: it attracts man to perform his basic duty of honouring his Creator, to keep in use his spiritual powers, and to exercise the necessary virtues of faith, hope and charity; it gives him the privilege of speaking directly with God and with Christ and of asking for what he desires— an intimacy that must in time correct and elevate man's whole spiritual life.

3. *The Necessity of Prayer in the Life of a Priest*

If, then, prayer is so important and so necessary, is it not extraordinary to hear on all sides: " I find it so

[1] Homily II, on Prayer.   [2] Homily XXX, on Genesis.

hard to pray. My prayers are so poor and so distracted. When I have been on my knees but a few
minutes it seems like an hour. I know it ought not to
be so, and yet I do not seem able to help it"? All
confessors must have had this said to them many times,
and most of them would have had to own that it was
true in their own case. But if this is so, there must
be something radically wrong. It would not be difficult to give a long series of instances to prove that
the great spiritual leaders and workers have always
been distinguished by the importance which they have
assigned to prayer. We are painfully conscious, when
we read their lives, that, in spite of all our activities
and studies, we have need that someone should teach
us afresh the very principles of religious life and work.
For where prayer is strong and frequent, there the soul
is in health and prospers; where prayer is intermittent
and feeble, the whole life flags, moral duties begin to
wear a forbidding aspect, and even the practical
activities which at first seemed able to take care of
themselves, are found to lack the inward support without which they, too, sooner or later, must inevitably
fail. Study-circles and congresses, valuable as they are,
will not effect much for the honour and glory of God
if they do not make us all men of prayer. We, to-day,
are in great danger of putting the cart before the horse.
What we want, then, is to do what S. Francis de Sales,
or S. Vincent de Paul did for France, or what the
earlier Tractarians did for England—encourage priests
to pray.

In the first place, we should realise more clearly that
prayer is work. We have no difficulty in persuading
ourselves that prayer is preparation for work. But
how many of us to-day look upon prayer as a work in
itself, as the essential work of a priest? There is to-day

only one priest living the strictly enclosed life in the Church of England. If we really believed that the work of prayer is as important as the other duties of the priesthood, such as study or preaching, there would be many more. The determination of the Apostles was: "We will give ourselves continually to prayer and to the ministry of the Word " [1]—and in that order. " Let him call for the elders of the Church and let them pray," was the direction of S. James.[2] Surely that man can have little of the true spirit of a priest who has no longing to bear some part in the great ministry of prayer of our great High Priest.

Would indeed that more priests might realise that prayer is the first work to which they are called. There are others who may be qualified to undertake many parts of the work of a parish, but who will make good the losses that are incurred by an unprayerful priest? Bishop Wilberforce, in one of his Ordination addresses said: " Whilst we may find instances of success, and sometimes of great and unlikely success, in the ministry of those who have lacked every other qualification, there can, I believe, be no instances of a successful ministry which was not full of prayers." [3]

[1] Acts vi. 4.   [2] James v. 14.
[3] On this subject see Chautard, *L'Âme de tout Apostolat*, passim.

II. THE THEORY AND PRACTICE OF PRAYER

(An Historical Sketch from the Time of Our Lord to the Present Day)

By Harry Davis

The revelation of God in the Old Testament and His incarnation in the New have not only provided man with the means of formulating his duty of prayer, and examples of the way to fulfil it: the process has culminated in the production of the worshipping society, the Christian Church. In this body the Spirit of Jesus continues to exercise the religion of Jesus. All its aspirations are directed towards a God now apprehended primarily as the Father of Jesus.

If the history of prayer has a climax—and it is to history that the modern world looks by preference for the explanation of every object and every event—then it is to be found in the three hours' silence of Christ upon the Cross; but as the preparation for that supreme moment was manifold, so, too, has been the unfolding of its consequences. When Christians pray, as in all they do, they do so in the person of their Head—" through Christ our Lord." But no one Christian can hope to reproduce more than one aspect of the prayer, as of the life, of Christ. If we would seek to know what went on during the darkness on Calvary, we must look for our answer in the whole history of the Church. That is the reason for the *aperçu* which this chapter attempts to provide.

16

1. *Patristic Prayer*

There are to be found in the Bible, sometimes in germ and sometimes well defined, all the well-known characteristics of the various kinds of prayer as we know them in the text-books of the present day.

In the Old Testament there is a marked insistence on Adoration, even where it forms only the prelude to petition as the chief subject of the prayer offered. Vocal prayer perhaps reached its zenith under the Jewish dispensation; and it is significant how much of it was incorporated into Christian worship: yet examples of contemplative prayer appear already in the visions of Isaiah, Jeremiah and Ezekiel.

Of our Lord's prayer whole books could be written; we can notice only one or two points. Need it be said that it was contemplative in the widest sense of the term? Witness the Transfiguration, and the legitimate inference which may be drawn from whole nights spent in prayer. It was also in the highest degree simple. Witness the Agony in the Garden (" saying the same words ").

The main body of this chapter is to be devoted to the way in which subsequent Christian generations have worked out what was implicit in our Lord's life and teaching.

The Apostles' prayers become more and more Trinitarian as time passes on. They also reflect, at first (as was natural), the tendency to verbosity of Old Testament times. But the duty of making the whole life an expression of prayer or adoration comes to the fore in well-known phrases of S. Paul. This is obviously the first attempt at translating into practice " They ought always to pray . . ." S. Paul can also be cited, with S. John, as the first of Christian mystics. Both of them experienced what would to-day be called mystical phenomena. S. Paul was perhaps a Stigmatic. The emphasis placed by S. James on the need to correlate prayer and active works in the Christian life shows the existence of a problem that is the heritage of all the ages.

Such evidence as can be gleaned from the earliest Christian writers adds nothing to what has already been outlined. The long Eucharistic prayer in I. Clement is on similar lines to those of the Old Testament. The amazing conclusions drawn by the writer of II. Clement in his attempts at mystical interpretation are also indicative of meditation in our sense of the word. The "Passions" of the martyrs show the prayer of adoration in a very high form, but still, of necessity, "vocal."

S. Clement of Alexandria was the first writer to treat technically of prayer. Being a Christian Gnostic, he naturally attaches a primary importance to the intellect in prayer. For him, the perfect man is he who has attained to the perfect divine knowledge. A man will pray for whatever he sincerely desires or aspires after. But how are we to know whether our desires are in accordance with the will of God? For if they are not in accord with His will, their satisfaction will be an injury to ourselves and to others.

To know, therefore, what is the will of God is the preliminary to all true prayer. But to know the will of God is only possible through a perpetual converse with God. And this converse with God, Clement calls the real prayer of the Christian Gnostic. It involves a familiar contemplation of the Perfect Goodness in itself, and in its unceasing care for man's salvation, and therefore the vision of that perfection for which, in God's purpose, man's nature was destined. The prayer of the Gnostic is, therefore, a constant state; the converse with God, which it implies, must have become habitual.

Behind all his ordinary activity, the Christian Gnostic developed this sense of God's presence with us and in us. " Holding high festival in our whole life, persuaded that God is on every side present, we cultivate our fields, praising; we sail the sea, hymning; in all our conversation we conduct ourselves according to rule. The Gnostic is very closely allied to God, being at once grave and cheerful in all things: grave on account of the bent of his own soul towards the divinity, and cheerful on account of his consideration of the blessings of humanity which God hath given us." This is Clement's interpretation of " Pray without ceasing." Petition finds its place in Clement's scheme; but he sees that it needs specially clear and definite knowledge of the will of God, and the purpose of the Gnostic's training is to give us that knowledge. Clement categorically states that rule which we find repeated through the whole of the history of prayer—that we can only pray with certainty for things that are really good, the things that concern the soul; *i.e.*, petition meant, in Clement's time, primarily a request for spiritual food. Only later did the reference to physical needs find an acknowledged place in petition. The " knowledge " on which Clement lays so much stress was a knowledge, not of information about, but of acquaintance with God, a knowledge which becomes a renewing and transforming element in our lives. The " considerations " with which we are familiar in the ordinary three-point meditation are the direct descendants of Clement's teaching on this subject.

The next great development of the doctrine of prayer came two centuries later, with the advent of monasticism. It was out of an increasing desire to make prayer a reality that monastic discipline first arose in Egypt, the country most affected by Alexandrian theology. Although a popular expression of religion, yet it owed its inception to Gnostic (in Clement's sense) teaching; it was only one more attempt to translate into action " Pray without ceasing."

For Cassian prayer was the whole art of life, not merely a series of occasional acts. The perfect life constitutes the perfect prayer, and life itself will never be perfected save through prayer. Hence the withdrawal of the early hermits to the desert. Cassian lays great importance on the purifying of the soul from all sin as a primary necessity for all real prayer. These early hermits also emphasised humility as being the root of all prayer and the indispensable condition of progress in the Christian life.

In accordance with their vocation, Cassian and his followers limited manual work to that which was needful to support life, and no more. Among the Egyptian hermits, we find the conception of the contemplative life pushed to the extreme limit. It could not be lived in community, but only in a hermitage, since the former militated against the attainment of full contemplative purity. " The heavenly transports experienced in solitude and the sublimity of contemplation are lost by return to the monastery." Anything that withdraws the hermit from the precincts of his cell and compels him to go out to work in the open air dissipates the concentration of his mind and all the keenness of the vision of his aim. Agricultural work is incompatible with the contemplative life, because the multitude of thoughts generated by such work makes unbearable the long silence of the hermit's cell.[1] It is at once evident that the three great cenobitic founders, Pachomius, Basil and Benedict, all turned away from the idea of a contemplative life such as this, when they made

[1] S. Thomas Aquinas remarks, in one of the *Quaestiones Quodlibetales*, that it is, " to say the least, inconvenient to recite Office while planting cabbages."

agricultural work an integral part of the monastic life they instituted.

We might perhaps say that the ideal of contemplative life that grew up in the East meant the absence of all active work; whereas the contemplative life in the West meant the presence of contemplative prayer in active work.

In the East the contemplative life developed on the lines laid down by Cassian—*i.e.* it was a life wholly given over to prayer; while in the West the type of contemplative life which grew up is best described by the word " mixed," *i.e.*, Western mysticism admitted a greater amount of work—intellectual or manual—in the lives of its devotees. It is the life inaugurated by S. Benedict.

In the course of the growth of monastic life there was evolved the Divine Office. This bears witness to the large place which vocal prayer held in the life of the Church of that period (as the commentaries of the Fathers on Holy Writ show), the employment of " discursive Meditation." But in tracing the history of our subject, the larger part of our space must be given to " Contemplative Prayer," for this was the kind of prayer which fascinated the masters of spirituality. The Easterns seem to have touched the two extremes—either they were contemplatives after the mode of Cassian, or they recited enormous quantities of Vocal Prayers. The distinctive type of Western spirituality took a middle course. It is the kind of contemplative life with which we are most familiar to-day.

S. Augustine is noteworthy in developing the preparation for prayer outlined by Cassian. He dwells on the need for mortification, or ascetism. To him, also, can be ascribed the notion of dividing the spiritual life into the purgative, illuminative and unitive ways, though the nomenclature is that of later writers.[1] Augustine, like most of the writers of his period, was steeped in Neo-Platonism, and his mysticism is therefore of a transcendental type.

We have now definitely reached the period when a life of prayer is quite clearly distinguished from a life in the world. Much is made of the comparison between Martha and Mary, and Augustine assigns to the contemplative life a superiority over the active life in the world. In noting this, we must remember that Augustine, in common with the great Western tradition, here means the " mixed "contemplative life—mixed, though pre-eminently a life of prayer. A further point emerges at this stage, with the notion that all, both religious and seculars, are called to the contemplative life, and that it is possible for all to rise to the heights of prayer described by S. Augustine.

To prevent misunderstanding, it is as well to remind ourselves that by contemplation or mysticism (words interchangeable) the writers with whom we are dealing mean what we know as active or acquired contemplation. So much is this prayer honoured that Gregory makes the practice of it a *sine quâ non* for all candidates for the pastoral office. The purely contemplative life, even as in the West we know it, lay outside Gregory's horizon.

2. *Pre-Tridentine Prayer*

There evolved two types of this contemplative prayer. On the one hand there are the transcendental mystics whose prayer was a stretching out of the soul to the infinite God, born of the mystic's sense of his own littleness and ignorance in comparison with the greatness of

---

[1] S. Thomas, following Augustine, prefers to speak of " beginners, proficients and the perfect."

the Godhead which he has perceived, of the total difference in *kind* between the divine and everything else.
Awe and self-abasement govern his outlook. To this
group of feelings we owe all negative ideas of the
supreme reality. This type of prayer is congenial to the
Neo-Platonic world-view, and hence it flourishes in the
early centuries. S. Paul, S. Augustine, S. Gregory, S.
Bernard and, later, Angela of Foligno, the " Cloud of
Unknowing," and the pseudo-Dionysius all exemplify
it. " *Abyssus abyssum invocat* " is its keynote.

On the other hand, there are those who find the goal
of their spiritual pilgrimage in the contemplation of
God dwelling within them. S. Teresa is the classic
example. This type of prayer is governed by the love
which casteth out fear, by a sense of the nearness, sweetness and intimacy of the Divine. It is an attitude of
joy, confidence and affection. These contemplatives
tell us of their attainment of That which Is as the closest
and most joyous of all communions, a coming of the
Bridegroom, a rapturous immersion in the uncreated
Light. They learn the secret of the universe not by
knowing but by being. Such contemplation is an
adorable friendship. Suso, the two Catherines, Julian
and Mechthild of Magdeburg carry on this tradition.
Many contemplatives present both aspects of the
mystic way,[1] but it is worthy of note that the advent of
the immanentist philosophies of the sixteenth century
and after coincides with the chief of this class of mystic.

We have mentioned here—rather out of place—the
lines on which contemplative prayer develops, so as to
avoid a continual return to details later on.

To return to the historical sequence: in S. Bernard

---

[1] Cf. S. Teresa's: " All is nothing: and God is All," and that
word of our Lord to S. Catherine of Siena: " I am who am: thou
art who art not."

and the Victorines, especially in the latter, there appears the enumeration of the steps by which the mind ascends to God: thought, meditation, the lower contemplation, the higher contemplation.

Apart from this and other minor elaborations, the masters of this pre-Scholastic period base their ideas on the teaching of Augustine and Cassian (the search by the soul for the ultimate truth). But another conception of the contemplative life had been introducing itself among the Benedictines since Benedict of Aniane, and it reached its limit in the Cluniacs of the eleventh and twelfth centuries. This took the form of a great increase in the celebration of masses and offices, so that these took up the greater part of the waking hours, to the exclusion of all else. This manner of life—spent mostly in church—came to be looked on as realising the ideal of the contemplative life. (In a curious twelfth-century dialogue between a Cluniac and a Cistercian, the Cluniac twits the Cistercians for spending most of their time in the fields.) The Cluniac ideal became the current idea of the contemplative life in Benedictine circles and beyond them for several centuries. S. Bernard and the Cistercians provided the corrective, and by restoring manual work in the fields enabled the monks to make progress in mental and contemplative prayer.

S. Bernard carries the theory of prayer a step forward. Hitherto the end of the contemplative life has been regarded as union with God; Bernard introduces the idea of spiritual fecundity, carrying on the imagery of the spiritual marriage. Thus there arose the zeal for souls which, in the true mystic, is not so much an interesting alternative to contemplative prayer, as an impulse derived from the mystical experience itself. It impels the soul to leave its quiet and go forth to bear spiritual offspring to its Lord. Once enunciated, this idea became a passion with many mystics—S. Teresa, S. Catherine of Genoa, Richard of S. Victor, S. Francis —as it had been with S. Paul.

About the time of S. Bernard there comes a very marked change in the kind of contemplation practised in the West. The reason for this is the immense influence which the writings of Pseudo-Dionysius began to exert. They had been translated into Latin by Erigena, and their ideas came into general vogue in the twelfth century. Dionysius laid great emphasis on the trans-cendence of God, and pushed to its extreme limit the " negative way " of attaining to knowledge of God. His theological conceptions are apparent in the German Dominican mystics of the fourteenth century, Eckhart, Tauler, Suso; also in Ruysbroeck, S. John of the Cross, Blosius and Fr. Baker. For Dionysius the soul in con-templation is borne up to the " ray of the divine dark-ness," and this, together with his other conceptions— including much that he has to say about the deceits of the devil in prayer—is diametrically opposed to the endeavours of the pre-Dionysian masters, who fix their gaze by preference on the " ray of unencompassed light."

The close of the patristic period, therefore, marks the end of a distinct school of contemplation, since all the ensuing writers are indebted to Dionysius. Apart from the extreme position of Cassian, and before the advent of Dionysius' influence, what was the characteristic note of the prayer of the Fathers?

1. It is stamped by its entire freedom from the influence of Dionysius, whose ideas and nomenclature are familiar to us in the great modern treatises on prayer.

2. It is pre-scholastic. Though the Patristic writers discourse on contemplation when occasion arises, they make no attempt at any systematic presentation of their

teachings in the form of a scientific treatise. A specu-
lative and philosophical treatment of the subject was
yet to come. The Fathers merely describe as best they
can their own experiences.

3. It is a prayer devoid of revelations and visions, so
familiar in later times, with SS. Gertrude, Mechthild of
Magdeburg, Mechthild of Hackborn, Bridget, Catherine
of Siena, Margaret Mary. (From SS. Peter, Paul, John
onwards there have been men who have seen visions,
but far more often it has been women who have had the
more elaborate pictorial visions.) The absence of
anything like this is a mark of early and patristic prayer.

4. Similarly, the psycho-physical concomitants of
rapture which are the common experience of the later
mystics are absent here. The type of contemplation
dominant in the West from 550 to 1150 is objective and
empirical, far removed from any kind of Quietism, and
consists solely in the endeavour of the soul to mount to
God in prayer and seek union with Him and surrender
itself wholly to His love—in the simplest meaning of
those words.

In passing, we must notice the devotion of the Rosary,
introduced in the thirteenth century as a means of
popularising some sort of simple pictorial meditation for
the unlearned.

With the Victorines, and more especially in S.
Thomas, mysticism tended to become a science of contemplation rather than contemplation itself, an intellectual system rather than a religious experience.

The ideas that had up to this time been expressed
were worked out by S. Thomas with his accustomed
thoroughness. He himself favours the mixed life, and
stresses the intellectual side of contemplation, being so
far in line with S. Augustine. S. Thomas stands at the

beginning of the golden age of mysticism. Until about the year 1500 there is a steady succession of writers who, though introducing no new thoughts beyond those of Dionysius, develop the ideas of the pioneers. Some dwell on the transcendental aspect of the mystic life, and others on its immanentist aspect; frequently both are spun together in one thread. The " Mirror of Simple Souls," Eckhart, Tauler, Suso, Ruysbroek, à Kempis, Hilton, Julian, and the two Catherines show us the mystical marriage combined with a sane and vigorous life.

3. *Post-Tridentine Prayer*

The next development of the prayer life comes after the Council of Trent; and in some respects it marks a change. It was an age of formulæ, whether plotting out the Seven Mansions of the Soul or the Thirty-Nine Articles of the Church of England. The writers are largely engaged in charting the seas of spiritual experience that their forefathers had discovered. Though the distinction between active and passive contemplation had been drawn in the fifteenth century by Denis the Carthusian, it now emerges as a common doctrine for the first time, and still provides a never-failing source of argument for the *illuminati* of to-day. Passive contemplation and mystical phenomena were by no means unknown to the patristic writers, but, in the inchoate state of the subject in their day, the precise limits of the capacity of the soul, aided only by the ordinary graces given to every man, were never recognised, much less defined. When the early writers spoke of the contemplative life being possible for every man, they were referring to an advanced state of the prayer of simplicity, and cared nothing whether or not it was accompanied by visions, auditions and the like.

C

Now, from the sixteenth century onwards, the whole field is mapped out. S. Ignatius, though familiar with the highest forms of prayer, is pre-eminently the doctor of discursive meditation. The immense difficulties of prayer and the temptations that beset the soul in the pursuit of its highest good were the special study of S. John of the Cross. Indeed, his distinction between the night of the senses and that of the spirit first drew attention to the " spiral " progress of the soul in its search for God. Viewed as a writer on the unitive life, he represents a regression to the Eastern type, since he wishes the true contemplative to forsake all other occupations. One of the most interesting things about S. John is his rooted distrust of those visions and revelations by which the mystics were beginning to set such store. To him it seems difficult to find a guarantee of their divine, or against their diabolic, origin. In his writings (as also in those of all this school) there is found that continual insistence on the necessity of mental prayer and that comparative depreciation of vocal prayer which is characteristic of the sixteenth- and seventeenth-century revival. This was probably motived by the knowledge obtained from the bitter experience of their disciples as to how easily continual repetition of vocal prayers in the cloister might empty them of all content. But apart from this, all the masters of this subject hold that prayer at its height dispenses with words and becomes a rapt and sustained contemplation of the divine nature.

The spiritual lore of S. John is largely concerned with the habitual preparation of the soul for its acts of prayer. In the forefront of this preparatory discipline he places what all the great mystics, and among them the English Quakers, have called " waiting upon God." Like S. Bernard, he stresses the fact that the things we ask for must always be qualified by the condition—" if they are according to the will of God." In the succession of immanentist mystics stands the well-known figure of Brother Lawrence, showing the passive tendency of French mystics in its sanest form.

Together with S. Peter of Alcántara, SS. Teresa and John form the basis on which modern spirituality has been erected. It was by taking the various points of these writers and developing them on their own lines that its different schools of thought arose. Thus the basis of the Salesian School is the offering of sacrifices, however small. The Bérullians, and the French school in general, make their chief devotion to God Incarnate in Jesus Christ, and dwelling in our souls. These ideas are familiar to-day in the works of Abbot Marmion.

In passing, we must notice the Quietism of the seventeenth and eighteenth centuries. Its best-known exponents are Molinos and Mme. Guyon. The error of this teaching lay in its depreciation of all active work and the small importance ascribed to the will. It exaggerated the function of pure love, going so far as to make of it the only virtue, whereas in reality it is the end, and not the beginning of spiritual progress. In consequence of this, we have the unfortunate attitude summed up in the phrase: " Leave God to act." As we know, this merely opened the way to laxity of all descriptions.

Perhaps one of the chief features of present-day teaching on prayer is the way the primitive ideas of contemplation are coming into their own. We are now sufficiently remote from the academic discussions consequent upon the Teresian reform to recognise the general and fundamental truths of prayer that the reformers were trying to make plain; and though there are still with us Mgr. Farges and Canon Saudreau to keep alive the warfare of the pen, both of these authorities, together with other representative writers of the day—when their technical terms are eliminated—agree in promoting the use of active contemplation as the ideal to be aimed at by all who seek to know the unsearchable riches of Christ. It is this, I think, that Louismet means, in spite of the ambiguous title of his *Science of Prayer*, where, having coined the phrase " Prayer of Faith " and equated it with all the various phases of the prayer of simplicity, he endeavours—by getting free from the terms which have been the subject of so much debate—to present active contemplation as the ordinary goal of those who tread the paths of the illuminative and unitive ways.[1]

To conclude: Is there any dominant concept which runs through the whole of this history? Such an one, I think, can be found in that of " search." Search after God in His essence, if haply we might feel after Him and find Him—a search which demands the most strenuous efforts and the most rigid self-discipline, yet one which is buoyed up by the certainty of success—a success guaranteed by the Resurrection of our Lord:

" *Dic nobis, Maria,*
Quid vidisti in via ? "

—but one which can have only a partial fulfilment in this realm of time and space. It is a search for the ulti- mate realities of that Fatherland to which we all belong by virtue of our Baptism. A search made not in the interests of academic inquiry, but in order so to live in the earthly house of this tabernacle that when it comes to its appointed end, the life to come shall be found to be but a vast expansion of that which has been to some degree developed here. In this sense all the adoration that has been offered by all the saints through all the

[1] See Abbot Butler, *Ways of Christian Life*, p. 232 n.

ages—adoration under cover of which they have unconsciously conducted their search—can be fitly summed
up in the immortal words of S. Bernard:—

> " *Jesu, spes pœnitentibus,*
> *Quam pius es petentibus !*
> *Quam bonus es quærentibus,*
> *Sed quid invenientibus !*
>
> *Nec lingua valet dicere,*
> *Nec littera exprimere ;*
> *Expertus potest credere*
> *Quid sit Jesum diligere.*"

III. THE SCIENTIFIC CLASSIFICATION

By Sidney Panton

THIS third chapter sums up a portion of the results which scientific study has gleaned from the historic process described in the preceding chapter. Ascetic theology is a science; but it is the science of an art, and a science of life; and therefore the order in which it chooses to classify the forms of prayer is the order of the stages of a typical life of prayer. The supernatural life, like the natural life, has its stages of childhood, of adolescence, of maturity; and though no two souls may have the same rate of growth, all show roughly the same sequence of stages. In one the features of maturity may show themselves early, in another the features of adolescence may persist into maturity; but we recognise these divergences from the normal just because we have a norm.

Scientific ascetic theology, then, presents its results as the conclusion of the induction made in *descriptive* and *historical* ascetic theology, which has the process of revelation and the lives of the saints for its field. It is an empirical science, and its methods are the methods characteristic of the biological sciences.

This might lead us to expect to find in the ontogenetic process, which it describes, the reproduction in little of the phylogenetic process traced in the preceding chapter. Any such *a priori* expectation is doomed to disappointment. There is no real evolutionary race-progress in sanctity. The sanctity of a Thérèse of Lisieux may be different from, but it is not higher than, the sanctity of a Teresa of Avila; for both are approximations to the same model, and can never be more than approximations. The saints really are to their Master in the relation in which the poets of the Augustan age fancied they stood towards Homer. We do not find vocal prayer alone under the Old Testament, mental prayer under the New, acquired contemplation in the Middle Ages, and infused in modern times. All are present in some souls at each period; and all souls in each period start from the same point; there may be more who reach the higher stages at one period than at another; there certainly is, as we have seen, a real progress in understanding of the typical process, the life-history of the Christian saint; there is a certain amount of progress in division of labour, and a certain amount of real innovation in technique: that is all we can say.

We have now to study the schematism of the typical process as the developed understanding of the ages displays it to us, before going on, in the second section of the book, to examine the great technical innovations, and returning, in the third section, to life in the raw, the growing soul, for whose sake technique and schematism alike exist.

We are concerned here only with the ordinary methods of prayer, as distinguished from mystical prayer. Such prayer, the prayer that is set before ordinary people as possible, or indeed expected of them, is comprehended in the two main divisions of Vocal and Mental Prayer.

1. *Vocal Prayer*

We start with a definition. Vocal prayer is that which is made by using words or signs, and, since we are considering Christian prayer alone, it must be added that these words or signs must be such as are generally approved by the Church.

It may be found generally true that all, except perhaps very advanced souls for whom the entire spiritual experience moves exceptionally, are drawn, not exclusively, but certainly predominantly, either to vocal or to mental prayer, but it is not advised by spiritual masters that either one or the other should be neglected entirely.

It is necessary, too, to give a definition of mental prayer, and we may use this one: " Mental prayer is an interior and silent prayer, by which the soul raises itself to God without the aid of words or formulæ, in order to discharge its duties towards Him and to become better."

It is, of course, possible for many souls, both in the religious state and in the world, to employ vocal prayer and find in it a ready and complete means of expression. It pays to God the homage not only of the heart but also of the body, and it makes use of words that have been hallowed by generations of very holy people, not only in Christian, but sometimes actually in pre-Christian times. Such forms must have a depth of meaning as well as a freshness that may well prove sufficient for very many. It is often found that in times of special need, as for example in dryness, long continued and severe, and notably in times of sickness and extreme weakness, vocal prayer is the only possible prayer. A large number of the martyrs under Henry and Elizabeth seem to have used in their agony brief vocal prayers based on our Lord's Name.

S. Teresa tells us that it is possible, as she knew, to rise to very great heights of contemplation from vocal prayer, but it would seem to be the more common experience that souls using vocal prayer generally move on from it until mental prayer comes to predominate.

The necessary thing is that the soul should be raised

interiorly to God. While this is achieved through vocal prayer no one should hesitate to employ it, but if and when it is found that the soul can best raise itself to God apart from words and phrases, it should do so. For this we have the authority both of S. Thomas and of S. Ignatius.

S. Ignatius, in his third method of prayer,[1] teaches a method of meditated vocal prayer in such a way that the simplest may use it, even while occupied in manual labour.

For all that it is possible thereby to attain to mystical contemplation, it is not as a rule recommended that any soul should be occupied exclusively with vocal prayer; and so we find S. Francis de Sales teaching that " if during vocal prayer you feel your heart drawn and invited to interior or mental prayer, refuse not to follow this attraction, but allow your thoughts to flow freely in that direction, and be not troubled at not having finished the vocal prayers which you had intended to say; for the mental prayer which you will make in their stead will be more agreeable to God and more useful to your soul." [2]

2. *Mental Prayer, Discursive, Affective and of Simplicity*

1. *Discursive.*—Of this first division there is no need to say much, for this form of prayer is familiar enough under the name of Meditation. All three forms (discursive, affective and the prayer of simplicity) are alike in that they are essentially active and not passive, *i.e.* the supernatural is latent in them, and they are elicited by efforts of the intellect, the will and the affections, in varying degrees as the soul advances in capacity.

At the bottom of the ladder of mental prayer there is the rung of discursive prayer. It is not a part of this

---

[1] See the following chapter.
[2] *Devout Life*, Pt. II. chap. i, n. 8.

chapter to suggest reasons for the difficulties experienced in offering this prayer, but we should note the importance of the part played by the reason in it. Whatever the method used, this will be found to be so. We make our preparation and then proceed to reflection of some sort. This is the use of the reason, in the course of which we try to look at the theme from various angles and in connection with various needs of which we are aware. All this reasoning helps the soul towards the real prayer which is to follow in the form of affections, petitions and resolutions. But at this stage the soul is not capable of arriving at the latter without the preliminary use of the reason.

2. *Affective.*—As advance is made, the soul is drawn to a more simple form of prayer. We have emphasised the use of the reason in discursive prayer, pointing out its place in the production of the essential prayer itself. In due course the soul learns to shorten the reasoning part of the method, and in time to dispense with it altogether. It is then able to pass quickly to the offering of the affections. The way to reach affective prayer, therefore, would seem to be the way of detachment. If the soul is living a detached life, it will be readily able to pass to the claims and beauties of Almighty God, and will not find it so necessary to go first through a process which really amounts to the careful removal of the hold of creatures on the soul. In such prayer it is necessary only to choose a subject and come with it into the divine presence. The soul is then readily moved to acts of love, gratitude, humility or similar affections. This form of prayer may close, as discursive prayer does, with a resolution; but it is better to keep to the same resolution for some period, in order to cultivate with more steadiness and success one virtue at a time.

3.—*Prayer of Simplicity.*—The name of this prayer indicates its nature. We have seen how the soul as it advances is able to diminish preliminaries which at first were essential to its prayer. They are so many devices to raise it to the level required for contact with its Maker in prayer. Later the soul is already, almost habitually, at this level, and such aids are no longer needed. First the intellectual part can be shortened, and the soul is able to be content with just a thought, a memory, the merest glance, after which it can get to God with its real self.

Later on even the affections are simplified. Whereas, before, the soul spent time—most of the time, in fact—in acts of love, gratitude, and so forth, elicited as the result of the various considerations made to start with, now it is content with God Himself. Before, it might proceed to elicit acts of love successively on account of creation, on account of grace, on account of the Church, on account of the saints, on account of its preservation, on account of God's long-suffering, and so forth. There was need for the soul to help itself to such acts by means of these considerations, and that, too, was the way to help it towards perseverance.

But now these acts, in such extended form, become an embarrassment, a fatigue, a check. The soul has become content with God, and needs no helps to realise His beauties. It is able to see, and to dwell on Him quickly, and such prayer has therefore been called, very expressively, the prayer of simple regard.

It is the prayer of Active Contemplation, and it has been summed up in these few words: "The soul looks and it loves." It is no longer the toilsome work of the imagination, the memory and the understanding. The soul gets straight to its goal, with a simple look.

Such prayer is the result of knowledge. We cannot love God if we do not know Him and know that He is lovable. But it is also the result of the realisation that God is all-sufficient, the primary object of the soul.

The things of God are secondary. The soul is charmed
by His own beauty and His goodness. It can then not
help but love.

There are two kinds of contemplation: the acquired
and the infused. Acquired contemplation is a state of
prayer into which a person may raise himself by his own
efforts, assisted of course by the graces granted in prayer;
it is sometimes transitory and sometimes habitual.
Such contemplation as we are considering is not the state
of mystical contemplation, and for the difference we must
refer to what was remarked earlier in this chapter, to
the effect that this form of prayer, like all the forms that
have been mentioned, is essentially active, and not passive. Mystical contemplation is also a prayer of a simple
loving look, but in it the soul is passive,[1] and what is
realised in it is received direct from God, and is not the
result of any immediate action on the part of the soul
concerned. In the prayer of simplicity the soul is in
action, and not only receiving what is vouchsafed to it.
It is active prayer arrived at its final development.[1]

[1] Cf. Jacques Maritain, *De la Vie d'Oraison* (Paris, 1924), Note III.
" On peut remarquer . . . que dans l'article où il distingue la grâce
opérante de la grâce co-opérante (I–II, III, a.2.), Saint Thomas
formule un principe général qui constitue la première racine théo-
logique de la doctrine de Saint Jean de la Croix sur la passivité de
l'âme sous l'action divine. Il y a, dit-il, des effets de la grâce dans
lesquels notre âme est mue, et ne se meut pas, et où Dieu seul la
meut, *effectus in quo mens nostra est mota, et non movens, solus autem Deus
movens*; alors c'est à Dieu que l'opération est attribuée, et en ce cas
la grâce est dite *opérante*, tandis que lorsque notre âme est mue et se
meut elle-même à la fois l'opération est attribuée non seulement à
Dieu, mais aussi à l'âme, et la grâce est dite *co-opérante*. A la
première catégorie d'effets appartient l'acte intérieur de la volonté
(c'est à dire le premier acte, auquel elle ne peut se mouvoir en
vertu d'un acte antérieur); quant à cet acte, la volonté se comporte
comme mue, et Dieu comme mouvant, *voluntas se habet ut mota, Deus
autem ut movens*, en particulier lorsque la volonté commence à vouloir
le bien, ayant auparavant voulu le mal."
The whole note is to be read.
(The literature dealing with this aspect of the science of prayer is,
of course, immense. The beginner might do worse than consult
Lehodey, *Ways of Mental Prayer*, or Steuart, *A Map of Prayer*.)

PART II

SOME METHODS OF PRAYER

I. THE IGNATIAN METHODS OF PRAYER

By Philip Bacon

Teaching on prayer has a history, just as has the practice of prayer. So in this second section we shall find, as we found in the first, analytical and historical elements. The first teaching of vocal prayer is a matter in which Christian mothers are competent to direct; the teaching of mystical prayer is the province of the Holy Spirit; and this book is primarily intended for the guidance of directors. Therefore this second section is concerned only with ordinary mental prayer, of which the most typical exercise, and that in which direction can play the greatest part, is discursive meditation. The two pre-eminent " classical " methods in this type of prayer are those known respectively as the Ignatian and the Sulpician or Oratorian. To these the teacher in search of a method will presumably first have recourse. But there are others; and should he find neither of the above-mentioned systems congenial to his pupil, or himself, he should know where to turn for an alternative. A complete exposition of all known methods would be exhausting as well as exhaustive; and it is unnecessary, since each differs but little from the next, and a gradation can be discerned among them, which is itself due to the historical influence of one school on another. The methods of S. Ignatius and of S. Sulpice are themselves not without historical connections, and accordingly, after the didactic exposition of the two methods in this and the following chapter, these connections are examined, and finally the picture is completed by some slight notice, at once historical and analytical, of other and less widely influential methods. This treatment of the subject seems best adapted to provide the director with the means of making his own selection and combination of elements, or at least of showing him where to go for them.

Of all methods of prayer, that of S. Ignatius stands first. The methods of Mauburnus and Cisneros and Gerard of Zutphen were actually a little earlier in date, but even chronologically it is very nearly true that the method of S. Ignatius is first.[1] And of the renowned methods of prayer, certainly his is first in time and foremost in importance. For the purposes of this study we may assume that of Ignatian prayer the *Spiritual Exercises* are the familiar example. Their importance lies in the fact that they are evidently the product of a supernatural revelation added to a deep personal experience. S. Augustine's *Confessions* and Bunyan's *Grace Abounding* are autobiographical; and the *Spiritual Exercises*, without being a relation of the Saint's inner life, are really just as much a revelation of it as are the works of the authors just quoted of theirs. And yet there is much more than that. It is traditional teaching that it was our Lady who revealed the *Spiritual Exercises* and the Constitution of the yet unborn Company of Jesus to S. Ignatius in the cave at Manresa, so that they are primarily a " ghostly showing " of God. " Thou spakest some time in vision unto thy Saints."

Perhaps it may surprise some to learn that one of

[1] The literature of Ignatian origins is so much more widely diffused, and the Jesuit spirituality itself so much better known in England than that of the French school, that no attempt is made here to enter into such questions as will be found discussed in the following chapters, where the respective contributions of Bérulle, Olier, and outside sources to the Sulpician method are assessed. [Ed.]

the leading characteristics of S. Ignatius was his expansive and elastic mind. Too many are accustomed to
assume that his method represents the instruments of
precision in spirituality—strong and rigid and accurate—
and do not look to it for flexibility and suavity or the
adaptability of life. Its true aspect can easily be missed
by a reader who does not grasp that the *Exercises* are
not to be understood by being read, but by being
performed; being performed, that is, with the personal
oral direction of a skilled guide.

To illustrate this, we may note that in one of the
Annotations (the eighteenth) the Saint lays it down
that: " These Spiritual Exercises ought to be adapted
to the disposition of those who wish to make them, that
is to say, according to their age, education or capacity."
This matter of adaptation is not very easy, and an
essential qualification for anyone who would attempt it
is that he should have a complete mastery of the exercises in their entirety and normal form. The *Directory*
insists that everyone entering the Society of Jesus must
make the Exercises completely and according to the
form laid down in the book . . . exactly as they stand.
Later they should go over the same ground several
times . . . because they will hereafter have to give
the exercises to others . . . they ought to have first
acquired a thorough and profound knowledge of them.
In the Anglican Communion, where retreats are short,
very few have the opportunity to make the Exercises in
their full length. Therefore a retreat-conductor among
ourselves does well, in giving a retreat, not to attempt
any modification (except shortening) till he has had
experience of giving or receiving some fifty retreats of
anything less than a week, according to this method.
But one retreat of a fortnight will teach him more than
many of a few days each.

D

But we must not dwell only on the use of the Exercises in retreat. To deal adequately with Ignatian prayer, this study should explain what is usually meant by the term " Ignatian prayer " without reference to retreats. We may wonder whether S. Ignatius himself understood the full use of the *Spiritual Exercises* when they were first revealed to him. He gradually found, in using them, and his disciples continued to find, the extent to which they are adaptable in the life of the Church. The Annotation quoted above makes provision for dealing with simple and illiterate persons and others who are not apt for making the Exercises, by outlining a much simplified form of retreat: and it is manifest that in his apostolic work among souls the Saint taught people who never made the Exercises in any form.

Apart from their use in retreat, the *Spiritual Exercises* contain many methods of prayer which can be used at other more ordinary times. First notice the exercises of self-examination. An insistence on the importance of self-knowledge was an integral part of the Saint's spirituality which he never failed to impress upon the Fathers of the Society itself and upon all his spiritual sons.

The Particular Examen, for eradicating a particular sin, fault or defect, is original and characteristic. It is to be carried out by retreatants every day of the retreat, while the *Directory* recommends that it shall be continued as a life-long practice.

This is rather part of the remote preparation for prayer than a method of praying, inasmuch as it aims at the acquisition of purity of conscience by the extermination of sins one at a time. The man who is desiring to make spiritual progress will decide which of his sins he will deal with first, and then will attack that

sin morning, noon and night. In the morning he will
commend his purpose to God, and at noon he will
review the position and mark with pencil and paper
the number of his surrenders since the morning. At
night he will do the same, and always with acts of
contrition and resolutions of amendment. The sight
of the number of dots stimulates a man to put forth
all his natural powers (a thing most men are slow to
do in spiritual matters) as well as to implore the grace
of God.

This examination of conscience three times daily
would seem morbid to anyone who did not understand
the method. (All Jesuits are trained in the use of this
examen, and it is enjoined upon them perpetually.
They have been charged with many things; but they
are not usually thought to be weak-minded through
excessive care of their consciences!) S. Ignatius
insisted very strongly on the use of the Particular
Examen by his Fathers, and went so far as to lay it
down that if for any reason it should be impossible for
one to make both meditation and self-examination on
any day, then it was meditation which was to be given
up rather than self-examination.

The General Examen can with greater truth be called
a method of prayer. It consists of a group of acts,
including among them the actual examination of conscience, the whole of which is to be performed every
day. The first point is to thank God for His benefits.
This is the complement or balance to the confession of
sin; for every day we are involved in a double series
of debts—on the one hand are God's benefits, for which
we owe Him at least acknowledgment, and on the other
hand are our daily sins, faults and imperfections which
throw us still further into His debt. The second point
is a prayer for light, seeing that the heart of man is

deceitful above all things and desperately wicked, and every man is blind in the matters which most concern him. The third point is the actual examination of thoughts, words and deeds.

The most noticeable point about the " General Examen for purifying oneself and confessing better " is this direction to examine first thoughts, then words, and then deeds. This is contrary to common practice, but it is manifestly the Gospel order—the order of the Sermon on the Mount.

The fourth point is a prayer for pardon, and the fifth a resolution of amendment, and the little exercise is closed by a Paternoster.

Still considering the subject of self-examination, attention should be directed to the First Method of Prayer, which is intended " to give a form, method, and some exercises whereby the soul may prepare itself, and may make progress in them, and in order that its prayer may be acceptable." How easy it is to assume that all prayer is indiscriminately acceptable! In this first method a man begins with an act of recollection which is outward as well as inward, and then, having asked the help of God, begins to consider one at a time the Ten Commandments, or the Seven Deadly Sins, or the Powers of the Soul, or the Five Senses, considering what is his practice in their regard, asking pardon for his defects and grace to amend. The time suggested for reflecting on each head is the time in which one might say three Our Fathers and three Hail Marys. The prayer ends with a colloquy to God our Lord according to the subject-matter. This method is a sort of combination of meditation and self-examination, with somewhat more than in the General Examen of the element of meditation; and, inasmuch as it partakes of the nature of meditation, it must come

under the proviso in the fourth addition of the First
Week: "In the point in which I find that which I
desire, there I will rest without being anxious to proceed
farther, until I have satisfied myself." This is an exercise
which S. Francis Xavier often enjoined on his penitents
in India.

Before coming to the supposedly complicated method
of Meditation which so many associate with the name of
Ignatius, I must mention two master ideas which in
this school of piety govern the life of the soul. Prayer
is not to be confined to oratory, chapel or church, nor
to services, meditation, contemplation or penance, nor
to solitude and quiet or to specific times: it must be
continuous. So the Saint lays down, in the constitu-
tions for his Society, that all should seek God in everything, ridding themselves as far as possible of all love
of creatures in order to spend all their love on the
Creator, loving Him in all His creatures and loving all
His creatures in Him, according to His most holy will.
That is to say, that whether studying or going for a
walk, or engaging in conversation, in everything they
see or hear or taste and in everything they do they
must try to see God. This principle of " seeing God in
everything and everything in God " governed the Saint's
own life, and he imposed it on his disciples. We can
find S. Ignatius' thought well expressed by Father
Jerome Nadal in the *Epistolae;* " Everyone treading
the path of prayer and of the spiritual life should strive
to find God in all his work and activities. The kind
of affection for prayer which seeks for continuous retire-
ment and solitude is not the sort of prayer which is
proper for this Company. What is right for us is a
prayer which stretches out to all the work and ministry
which is our vocation . . . the grace of Jesus Christ,
the enlightenment of the understanding, holy aspirations

and union with God should persist (even outside of prayer), and should coincide with all our actions, and guide them to such purpose that we find God in everything and so make all the day a feast unto the Lord." Ignatius told S. Francis Borgia, too, that it was a higher form of perfection to find God in everything and everywhere than to need an oratory and long prayers in order to get or maintain contact with Him.

The other governing idea or principle of the ascetic life is the excellence of the practice of the presence of God. This, along with the other, made it possible for the early Jesuit fathers to fulfil S. Ignatius' exacting demand that prayer should not necessarily be connected with solitude, but ought to continue in the very midst of work. His sons must not cease work nor must they cease to possess their souls in recollection of the presence of God. At the same time, he made it clear that no one could ever attain to familiarity with God who grudged retiring into solitude when necessary.

We have already said that there are many methods of Ignatian prayer, and perhaps have left the impression that meditation is only one of them. Actually the term " Meditation " covers some half-dozen methods. There is only one form described as meditation, but three of contemplation (which, as S. Ignatius uses the word, means what we ordinarily mean by " meditation "), and three methods of using all four forms. " Meditation," with him, is applicable in general to abstract subjects such as sin, pardon, judgment; and the name " contemplation " is used for the consideration of actual incidents of our Lord's earthly life.

The characteristic form of " Contemplation " is that of the contemplations of the Second Week in the *Spiritual Exercises*. It consists of Preludes, Considerations and the Colloquy. The three Preludes are short acts which, so to speak, dress the scene, bring the actors on the stage, play the overture and ring up the curtain. The first is a short act of memory by which the context of the incident is recalled, and the second an act of the imagination which is known as the " Composition of Place "; in which the exercitant pictures to himself the place, the road, the street, the country, the size and shape of the building, of the hills, the time of day, the temperature, the geology or anything of the sort which makes the scene real to him. The third is a short exercise of the affections, being a fervent prayer, " that I may have a more interior knowledge of our Lord Jesus Christ, who for me was made man, that I may the more love Him and follow Him."

Next follow the considerations; the work of the intellect. It is usual to consider the subject for contemplation in three points or divisions, *e.g.* in the incident of the healing of the lepers the divisions would naturally be: the lepers' appeal; Christ's response; the return of one only to give thanks. This working over the subject in the mind is meant to lead to acts of the affections and to produce some result in the will— " gather some fruit," is S. Ignatius' expression—so the considerations lead simply enough to the third part, the colloquy. This is described as being a converse as of friend with friend or servant with master; it is, like a conversation, impossible to define as to its subject-matter, because that arises out of the considerations; sometimes it will be to ask for some grace, and at other times to accuse oneself of some evil, to make known one's affairs, or to seek counsel; perhaps to make a resolution.

It is worth mentioning here that S. Ignatius is not one of those who suppose that every meditation or contemplation should issue in a resolution. At any rate, he does not demand a particular resolution; and usually, in his view, it would be a complete and well-made exercise which strengthened the resolve to do God's will whatever that might be. After the colloquy the contemplation is finished by the recitation of the Pater-noster or some other vocal prayer.

This outline of a contemplation is filled in in several ways, and we can scarcely be too grateful to a spiritual giant like S. Ignatius for crumbling his bread so that we lesser folk can feed with ease. His first method of dealing with the considerations is to divide each " point " once more into three and bid us consider the persons, what they are saying and what they are doing, and in each case seek to derive some profit. In the example of the ten lepers, the exercitant would first regard Jesus and His disciples and then the ten lepers, and reflect upon them. Next he would attend to what they are saying: " Jesus, Master, have mercy on us." " Go, show yourselves to the priests "; and reflect to derive some profit. And then he would regard what Jesus and the lepers are doing—*i.e.* Jesus and His disciples going into a certain town; ten lepers standing in a group afar off—and see what thoughts would arise from observing their actions. In a similar manner he would deal with the second point and with the third.

The second way of dealing with the points for con-sideration is known as the method of the Three Powers of the Soul, the Memory, Intellect and Will. In homely language we may say that this is to find answers to the questions, " What do I know about it? " " What do I think of it? " " What can I do about it? " on each of the " points " into which the subject is divided. It would be impossible to do this in strict order and without overlapping, for the three powers work con-currently, and when a man reasons he also remembers;

but it is natural to begin with memory and then set the intellect to work. The activity of the will cannot be confined, since it is the necessary operative principle even in remembering and understanding. In the end, especially in the Colloquy, affections are meant to take the place of deductions, and aspirations or resolutions the place of recollected facts. Here it is appropriate to quote from the Fourth Addition, that " in the point in which I find that which I desire, there I will rest without being anxious to proceed farther until I have satisfied myself." And from the Second Annotation: " It is not the abundance of knowledge which fills and satisfies the soul, but to taste and feel the matters interiorly." And so a meditation or a contemplation is not to be approached as if it were an examination-paper in which a certain number of questions must be attempted.

S. Ignatius is practical above all, and in every method of his prayer he is at pains to insist that the method is but a means, and the aim is to gather some fruit, to derive some profit. That is why men should be content when they succeed in obtaining what they desire, without striving to carry out further means which are directed to no further end. In the fable the hedgehog is all points but the sausage is all meat; and the Saint does not want—in fact, he fears—unnecessary elaboration. Yet there are some who need much help, and even combining " The Three Powers " with " Persons, Words and Actions," do not find the points too many.

Then there is a third method of meditating or contemplating, which is called " The Application of the Senses," and which is supposed to be the simplest of all methods (" very easy and useful," as the *Directory* says), though the question of its simplicity has for many years been a matter of hot debate. The explanation in the

Exercises mentions the ordinary preludes, which are the same as for the other methods, and then continues: "The first point consists in seeing the persons with the eye of the imagination, in particular meditating upon and contemplating their circumstances and gathering some fruit from the sight. The second point is to attend with the hearing to what they are saying or might say—and I will reflect with myself to derive some profit. The third is to smell and to taste the infinite sweetness and fragrance of the Divinity, of the soul and of its virtues and everything else according to the person contemplated. And I will reflect in order to gather some fruit. The fourth is to kiss, touch and feel the places which the persons contemplated tread or touch, always reflecting to gather some fruit." This method, like the others, concludes with a Colloquy and a vocal prayer.

We may be inclined to ask whether S. Ignatius does not indicate which of these methods is to be preferred. The best answer is to be found in such an observation as he makes in the Fourth Week—that the exercitant is to make use of light, or of seasonable enjoyments, as, for instance, in summer of refreshing coolness, and in winter of the warmth of the sun or fire—all this according as the soul thinks or conjectures that these things can help it to rejoice in its Creator and Redeemer. That is typical. S. Ignatius wants a man to make his own experiments. He indicates the end to be attained, gives directions, suggests methods, points out possible routes and gives examples of things which can be done. Then he says: "Look carefully, make your own choice, try these means for yourself. Then, when you have made your experiment, abide by the method which you find successful, and as to external aids, use them or ignore them according to whether they help you or

not. And never treat means as ends in themselves."
Unless you can interpret S. Ignatius according to his
own expansive and elastic spirit, you can never understand the range and power of his methods.[1]

At the end of the *Spiritual Exercises* are Three Methods
of Prayer, the first of which we have considered under
the classification of self-examination. The Second
Method of Prayer consists in considering attentively
the meaning of each word of a prayer. The preliminaries, which are the same for all three methods
of Prayer, are as follows:—

" Before entering on prayer let the mind repose a
little, either sitting or walking as shall seem best, considering meanwhile whither I am going and for what
purpose. Next, one or two paces from the place in
which I am about to pray I will stand for the space of
an Our Father with my mind raised on high, considering
how God our Lord sees me; and make an act of
reverence.

" The preparatory prayer will be made conformably
to the Person to whom the prayer is addressed.

" Then the person using this method, either kneeling
or sitting according to his preference and that in which
he finds more devotion, keeping his eyes shut or fixed
on one spot without letting them rove, will say the first
word of the prayer, *e.g.*, ' Our Father,' and reflect upon
it as long as he finds meanings, comparisons, relish and
devotion; and let him do likewise with each succeeding
word of this prayer or any other. Where a single word
does not make sense, several ought to be joined together.
This prayer is to be made without hurry or anxiety
to finish the consideration of the whole prayer; the
rest can always be left for another time."

[1] See A. Poulain, S.J., *The Prayer of Simplicity*, C.T.S., *passim.*
(chap. II. of the same author's *Les Grâces d'Oraison*).

The last of these methods is a recitation of a prayer in time, somewhat as in music. The preliminaries are the same as for the Second Method, and the actual prayer may be the same, *e.g.* the Lord's Prayer, the Hail Mary, the Salve Regina. But it is to be recited rhythmically—one word to a breath—and between the breaths particular attention is to be paid to the meaning of the word or to the Person who is addressed or (which seems curious) to the distance which separates such a high dignity and ourselves.

This is a useful method for humble souls and for more sophisticated ones in times of weariness, illness, business, temptation, excitement, overwrought nerves or overwork. Even very advanced souls have found solace at difficult times in such prayer. And less perfect souls can use it and say with good conscience, " I have done all that I can."

II. THE METHOD OF SAINT-SULPICE DESCRIBED

By REEVES PALMER

M. OLIER [1] divides mental prayer into three parts: the preparation; the prayer itself; and the conclusion. The preparation is threefold: remote, less remote, and proximate; the first being occupied in removing obstacles, the second in preparing what is necessary to pray well, and the third being as it were the entrance into prayer.

The more remote preparation may be said to extend over the whole of life, and is principally occupied with three *obstacles:* sin, the passions, and the thought of creatures.

The less remote preparation is concerned with three *times:* the time when the subject of prayer is given overnight; the time between then and waking in the morning; and the time from waking to the beginning of the prayer. The first requires attention, the second a review of the subject and strict silence, and the third the affection of love and joy with which we should approach prayer.

The proximate preparation is almost a part of the prayer itself. It comprises three acts:—

[1] The Sulpician method of prayer as approved by M. Olier is described in an appendix to E. H. Thompson's life of M. Olier, which is an abridgement of Chap. 15 of Fr. Faber's *Growth in Holiness*. This description is, in substance, that given here, on pp. 55–58 of this chapter.

1. The putting of ourselves in the presence of God.

2. The acknowledgment of ourselves as unworthy to appear in His presence.

3. The confessing ourselves incapable of praying as we ought without the aid of divine grace.

(For each of these M. Olier gave minute rules taken from ancient sources.) The body of the Prayer consists of :—

1. Adoration,
2. Communion,
3. Co-operation.

In the first, we adore, praise, and thank God. In the second, we try to transfer to our own hearts what we have been praising and loving in God, and to participate in its virtue according to our measure. In the third, we co-operate with the grace we are receiving by fervent colloquies and generous resolutions.

Adoration

In adoration we contemplate the subject of the meditation in Jesus, and worship Him on account of it, in a becoming way. Hence there are two things to be observed in this first point. Suppose, for instance, the subject be humility. We first consider Jesus as humble, and in this again are included three things: our Lord's interior dispositions of humility, the words He said, and the things He did. Secondly, we lay at His feet six offerings: adoration, admiration, praise, love, joy, and gratitude; sometimes going through all of them, sometimes selecting such as harmonise best with the subject of our prayer. This point is extremely important; first, since it leads us to contemplate our blessed Lord as the source of all virtues; and secondly, since it leads us to regard Him as the original exemplar of which grace is to make us copies; thirdly, because, of the two ends of prayer—the veneration of God and the petition of man—the first is the more perfect; fourthly, because, if we look to our own interests, of the two roads which lead to perfection—prayer and imitation—the first is the shorter, the safer and the more direct. "To dip our souls as it were in the dye of the Heart of Jesus by love and adoration, is a quicker way to imbue them with a virtue than multiplied acts of the virtue itself would be."

Communion

The second point is communion, by which we endeavour to participate in what we have been loving and admiring from the first. It contains three things. We have first to convince ourselves that the grace we desire to ask is important for us, and we should try to convince ourselves of this chiefly by motives of faith. The second thing is to see how greatly we are wanting in that grace at present, and how many opportunities of acquiring it we have wasted. The third and chief thing is the petition itself; and this petition may take any of four shapes; the types of which are found in Scripture:

1. Simple petition.

2. Obsecration, which is the adding of some motive or adjuration, as "By the merits of our Lord " or " By the graces of our Lady."

3. Thanksgiving; for thanksgiving for past graces is the most efficacious petition for new ones.

4. Insinuation; as when the sister of Lazarus said no more than: "Lord, he whom thou lovest is sick."

All these petitions must be accompanied by four

conditions—humility, confidence, perseverance, and the inclusion of others in our prayers; since our Lord teaches us to ask God for *our* daily bread, and to forgive us *our* trespasses.

Co-operation

The third point is co-operation, in which we make our resolutions. In these resolutions three things are required: they must be particular, present, and efficacious. They must be particular, because general resolutions are of very little use except in union with particular ones. They must be present, that is, we must have some application of our resolution present to our minds as likely to occur that day. They must be efficacious, that is, our subsequent care must be to carry them out with fidelity, and we must fully intend to do so by an explicit intention at the time we make them.

The Conclusion of our prayer consists in three things, all of which are to be very briefly performed. First we thank God for the graces He has given us in our prayer —the grace of having endured us in His presence, of having given us the ability to pray, and of all the good thoughts and emotions we have experienced. Secondly, we ask pardon for all the faults we have committed in our prayer—negligence, lukewarmness, distraction, inattention and restlessness. Thirdly, we must put all into our Lady's hands to offer it to God, to supply all defects, and to obtain all blessings. Then follows the spiritual nosegay of S. Francis de Sales, that is, some thought for the day to refresh us in the dust and turmoil of the world.

From this exposition of the dry bones of the method we pass to the living tissues which clothed them, and consider the theological emphasis characteristic of " Oratorian " or Sulpician prayer. A series of recently-delivered Bampton lectures [1] brings against post-Tridentine Catholicism the charge that it tends to displace true prayer by substituting meditation with a view to progress in virtue. This charge falls flat, as far as the Sulpician method is concerned. It is clearly possible to think of mental prayer as meaning no more than meditation, but this method is no party to such a mistake. Here the meditation proper (with or without the distributive use of the memory–understanding–will convention) forms the second part of the overnight preparation; and the three terms used to describe the body of the prayer—adoration, communion, co-operation—are, in themselves and in the directions given for them, terms of prayer pure and simple. Faber tells us that they are respectively equivalent to the picturesque phrases of the ancient Fathers: "Having Jesus before the eyes," "having Jesus in the heart" and "having Jesus in the hands." The body of the prayer is worship, and in it there are direct dealings with Jesus in person. It may be Jesus risen, Jesus crucified, Jesus enthroned, Jesus in Galilee, or in any other of the mysteries of his life for his friends.

Here, then, in the body of the prayer is Jesus. Bérulle, its original deviser, for his passionate attachment to the person of Jesus Christ, had well earned from Pope Urban VIII. the name of "Apostle of the Incarnate Word." "This servant of God and friend of the bridegroom," writes Père Bourgoing, "used to look upon and adore chiefly the divine person of Jesus Christ our Lord, united to our nature; that is to say, Himself considered in His personal state of life, in His divinely-human being; not only as God, nor as man so much; or in His humanity as such; but as being the God-Man, in His substantive state of life which includes His

---

[1] K. E. Kirk, *The Vision of God.*

E

splendours and His abasements, His filiation both divine and human in one and the same person, and the possession of the properties of the one and the other nature in the hypostatic union of God the Word." [1]

" This is an important point, for it is the basis and the subject-matter of all other mysteries. We celebrate the birth of the God-man, His manifestation or epiphany, His presentation in the temple, and all the other mysteries of the life, Passion, Resurrection and Ascension of this same Jesus, God and man, who is their author and their subject. These mysteries have passed and slipped away as far as their action and substance are concerned ; but the author and subject of these mysteries who embraces the grace, the life, the perpetual spirit of them, is abiding, and liveth eternally, as saith the Apostle—Jesus Christ the same yesterday, to-day, and for ever." [2]

Besides realising thus emphatically the abidingness of the grace-giving activity of the God-man which the mysteries display in single and transient examples, Oratorian teaching has much to say regarding the human side of the prayer-relation. The Son of God on earth teaches by example what it is to adore God, not merely by affection and desire, but by His state of being and relationship to Him. Corresponding to this divine filiation of the only-begotten Son of God to His Father, there is set up as between redeemed humanity and its Redeemer an adoptive filiation to the person of the Redeemer. Bérulle uses the text " Thine they were and thou gavest them me " to illustrate this (S. John xvii. 4). " It is necessary," he writes, " to learn from the state of the Son of God in regard to His Father,

[1] It is significant that Bérulle received Papal authorisation for the solemn feast of the Splendours of Jesus, and drew up its office— and that in the Oratorian devotion to the " Interior of Jesus " is found one of the sources of modern devotion to the Sacred Heart.

[2] Heb. xiii. 8.

what should be our state in regard to Him (Jesus Christ)." Of the two ways of serving Him—by *action* and by *state*—we are to learn, in imitation of the God-man's relation to His Father, to serve Him by state of being; to "embrace a manner of life which in itself does honour to the majesty of God, and is the source of holy, virtuous actions in honour of the state of life into which the Son of God has entered by the sacred mystery of the Incarnation and in which He persists eternally in the heavens." The conditions of Oratorian prayer-life are set up by the will to adopt this state of being in regard to God the Son, our Redeemer. For the God-man to become the father of the world to come, it was necessary for Him to change His state of being, and to enter the world of our being; for us to honour Him in our state of relationship to Him, it is necessary for us to change our world and enter His. This is the source of the type of prayer characteristic of the Oratory. Bérulle is careful to point out that many books on prayer do not seem to be in conformity with " our institution." Speech and imagination are apt to be a hindrance in making our prayer on some mysteries relevant to our life. " We need a way of prayer which we can use on all kinds of subjects, however great and elevated they may be."

" This manner of prayer consists in having the requisite dispositions of respect, honour and deference towards the subjects proposed, in abasing oneself before God, confessing one's worthlessness and powerlessness to penetrate these things by thought, contenting oneself with looking on them in humility, in order to honour and reverence them until it pleases God to look upon our lowliness and poverty, and to give us His light to understand these subjects. For this one will ask from time to time, without, however, undertaking to penetrate these things or to form thoughts about them unless God applies us to them by His Spirit; for it is the Spirit of God which opens the door to us, enabling us to enter into the understanding of these elevated subjects; ' The Spirit searcheth all things, even the deep things of God.' [1]

" We ought then really to have the disposition of a beggar in prayer; for just as the poor, after having knocked at the door, have to wait patiently until one brings them something, and afterwards begin to knock again, avoiding importunity, however; so the soul which realises its poverty and indigence, and more than that, sees that it deserves nought save hell for its sins, the soul, I say, ought to be mean and abased before the majesty of God, trying by all sorts of means to appease His anger and to draw upon His loving-kindness, whether by modestly knocking at the door of heaven by acts of humiliation and compunction, of realisation of its nothingness and of the majesty of God; or by waiting till it shall please God to come to the aid of its necessity, and to help it in its miseries.

" Again, one can hold oneself in the presence of God in the capacity of a very lowly slave, who, waiting with all humility and reverence to receive the commands of his Lord and Master, offers Him his whole heart and powers for anything which He wishes to do with him, and for all that He wishes him to do. This method should be followed, since, besides being of great utility to the soul, it honours God more than other methods of prayer which are customarily used. For we do not honour God, strictly speaking, by the thoughts that we form about Him and His mysteries—our thoughts are too low, too unworthy of His greatness—but by means of the interior dispositions of poverty and humility which it has towards God and towards His mysteries our soul does honour Him and glorify Him in some fashion,

[1] I. Cor. ii. 10.

since it shows submission, love, esteem, respect, reverence towards the greatness and majesty of God, so far as it can in the face of His exalted mysteries."

" It is true," Bérulle continues, " that this manner of prayer is not for all . . . beginners ought not to set themselves at the table of the bridegroom; it is, on the contrary, always needful for them to take the lowest place, and to wait that they may be found worthy to hear that holy word of the Lord: ' Friend, go up higher.' [1] For that reason it is needful to choose the lowest method of prayer. This method is meditation, but we ought not to bind ourselves to it in such a way that we cannot go out from it if God gives us attraction for something else; for it is right always to recall as a fundamental truth that prayer is a gift of God; that the Holy Spirit is the great Master of it, and that it is an art that one learns only by oft-repeated exercise."

[1] Lk. xiv. 10.

III. THE HISTORICAL ORIGINS OF THE
METHOD OF SAINT-SULPICE

By REEVES PALMER

THE method of prayer we have just considered is found succinctly drawn up as a scheme in the writings of M. Olier, the great reformer and parish priest of Saint-Sulpice. M. Olier had a genius for making things catch on among the ordinary folk; and this genius had two constituents. He not only used to popularise a good thing when he received it; he had that painstaking thoroughness of application whereby he translated his " good thing," whatever it was, into popular and practicable terms. He is incomparable as a liaison officer between the study and the street. Things thus became named Sulpician, not so much because of their origin, as by reason of their effective use in that wonderful parish of his. This is probably true of the catechetical method of Saint-Sulpice; it is certainly true of the method of mental prayer here called Sulpician. For it is also the method of S. Vincent de Paul; of Charles de Condren; of Père Bourgoing, the biographer of Bérulle; and, in our own day, of Father Faber and Cardinal Newman. In a word, it is *par excellence* the method of the Oratorian priests. Saint-Sulpice was but one of the results of the Oratorian revival; the congregation of S. Vincent de Paul another; the Eudist Congregation of Jesus and Mary, with its own variant of the method, yet a third; behind them all is the majestic figure of the Cardinal de Bérulle, their founder and spiritual father.

M. Olier really belongs to the second generation of Oratorians, having as his immediate instructor and confessor Père de Condren, who became Superior-General of the Oratory on the death of the Cardinal de Bérulle in 1629. There is a statement by Bérulle on the conception of the priesthood which indicates what it meant to become a priest under such auspices. Apparently someone had said that the priests of the Oratory were not obliged to live so holy a life as religious under vows. " What? " asked Bérulle, " would it be possible that our Saviour should desire so great a perfection in all the communities and that He would not require the same from His own order, which is that of the priesthood? For the priesthood is really the order which He Himself instituted in person—in a word, the order of His ambassadors, who speak in His name, act by His power, who bind and unbind souls, who open and shut the kingdom of heaven; so, while religious are consecrated by very praiseworthy and holy vows, priests are consecrated by the actual operation of Jesus Christ, an operation which imparts the Holy Spirit according to His words:—' Receive the Holy Ghost.' " [1] In these unstudied words Bérulle describes the conception of the priest's vocation which was dynamic for his life-purpose in France as it had been dynamic for S. Philip Neri in Italy. There are two other special places in Bérulle's writing, where the occasion demands that he show the bearing of this Foundation, to use S. Ignatius' word. The text of his little work for the direction of superiors is: " Ars artium cura animarum." This art of " writing in souls " is also a science; and the knowledge which this science utilises is neither philosophical nor theological,

[1] John xx. 22.

but spiritual. We are here touching not on the method of mental prayer, but on the genius of it. He gives its four principles in Chapter 12 of the pamphlet just cited, thus:—

" This is a knowledge which is bestowed by Jesus and likewise emanates from Jesus; it aspires to Jesus, and with the Apostle knows only Jesus and Him crucified; but in Him and in His cross it knows all things and reaches to the end of all things, namely to Jesus, the Alpha and Omega; for so He reveals and names Himself to the beloved disciple.

" Let all of you be amateurs of this truly spiritual science, of this science which has Jesus for its goal, for its object, and for its source; of this science which is only to be learned from Jesus, of this science which has for its principles (1) humility of spirit, (2) purity of heart, (3) self-abnegation, (4) union with Jesus."

But even more definite than the conception of the priesthood which inspired the life-purpose of the Oratorian fathers, is the series of observations on the interior life of the Oratorian priest in community which Bérulle made in drawing up the Rule of the Congregation of the Oratory. It is here that we find directions on mental prayer which are the foundation of distinctive " Oratorian " methods and principles of prayer.

He advises the priest in community:

1. " At least three times a day (e.g. when beginning prayer, during mass, and at some time after mid-day) to make a definite act of love to God; to make a definite oblation of himself, his life, his eternity, and his present working-day; and to make similarly three acts of special regard towards Jesus Christ, which three acts are called (a) adoration, (b) oblation, and (c) intention." It can hardly be doubted that the translation of this scheme into the three acts of the body of Sulpician prayer

(adoration, communion, co-operation) is a translation of ideas from the community to the parish, for the guidance of the Christian living in the world.

2. The same three acts are then advised in due measure in regard to the Virgin Mother of God " specially to honour her in her state of grace and dignity as Mother of God and in the sovereignty which corresponds thereto; to accept her as our sovereign Lady, on whom we ought to depend in all that concerns us."

3. Not to allow two hours' interval to pass without raising ourselves to Jesus Christ our Saviour by some act of love or adoration expressly made if we have the opportunity.

4. Further, not to allow any day to pass without our adoration, oblation and intention being actually and interiorly presented to Jesus Christ and to His holy Mother in some place expressly chosen. For " these three acts contain one of the greatest duties of our soul towards God, and one of the principal matters for which we are alive on earth."

Since now we find that " Sulpician prayer " is actually Bérullian in origin and conception, and that it is found in M. Olier and others just because they are faithful Oratorian priests, we are entitled to say that this conception of priesthood and this method of mental prayer are mutually interwoven at the source. One of the most interesting chapters in the history of the seventeenth-century spirituality in France here unfolds itself. It is the connection between Ignatian and Oratorian conceptions of mental prayer. It is possible to feel that M. Bremond [1] was a little unfortunate in his sharpening of an issue here and yet to feel grateful to him, rather than to his literary opponents, for drawing attention to a matter of real interest. We refer to the controversy

[1] H. Bremond, *Histoire Littéraire du Sentiment Religieux en France.*

only because the "calumnies" from which Bérulle suffered for ten years in silence, and which were ultimately silenced by his magnificent book on the Splendours of Jesus, centred round a particular word, or rather two interchangeable words—servitude, and oblation, as expressed in the two vows. That certain militant Jesuits were the occasion of the trouble seems historically incontestable; and it is at least suggestive that the major modification in the prayer-method as found in M. Olier's writings is the substitution of the idea and word "communion" between adoration and co-operation for Bérulle's own strong term, "oblation." (Olier also puts "co-operation" for "intention," but that is a distinction without a difference.) If, however, from the attitude of these militant Jesuits we deduce our idea of the relation between Ignatian and Oratorian principles, we start wrong. They must settle with their father-confessors—they are mere minnows beside Ignatius and Bérulle; and Bérulle, to do him justice, never thought they were anything else.

The true relationship of Bérulle to the Ignatian spirituality is one of affection and respect. As boy, youth and man, he was educated and experienced in the method of the Exercises. His first literary production, *On Interior Self-denial*, might have as its sub-title "A Study of the Idea of Detachment, in the manner of the Spiritual Exercises"; his vocational retreat at which he made his election was made at a Jesuit establishment under the direction of Père Magius. He entered it fully resolved to take Jesuit vows if God so willed; he followed faithfully the instructions of his director, saying naïvely: "I am here under a rule of obedience, and thus ought to let God assist me by this method rather than any other I might have chosen"; and also, "Acting contrary to my own will, I will desire that

God rather inclines and calls me to religious vows than to any other state of life."

All this establishes that in reality Bérulle owed an immense personal debt to those spiritual exercises on which his personality had been fashioned from early years, and no candid reader of his full writings could think otherwise. The real point of departure for Oratorian prayer-life is in the displacement of theological ideas which took place when, for the conception of the soldier of Christ on the war-path, the conception of the priest as the ministerial organ of the divine life and rule on earth is substituted. The soldier is dependent on his orders, but the priest on his relationship to the source of his priesthood. Hence while the positive acts of the memory, understanding, and will form the body of the prayer for members of the Society of Jesus, acts of the soul expressing adoration, servitude, union, *liaison*, adherence, to cite Bérullian terms, are substituted; furthermore, the whole thing is called an " elevation " rather than a meditation.

A probable factor assisting the evolution of the method is the experience of the Abbé de Bérulle as director-general of the houses of French Carmelites. There are preserved to us two hundred devotional addresses and conferences which Bérulle gave to the Carmelites to inspire their prayer, and the following short extract from a letter of direction reflects his ideals for their mental prayer. The text is from the temptation narrative : " He was with the wild beasts."

" Adore Jesus in these states of His. Refer (the interior abasement which) you are feeling to Him in an act of homage to this exile of His, this divine and adorable abasement of His in the view of the angels and of His holy Father. I beseech you to apply to your own soul and condition the grace and power of His interior

and exterior states, for the fulfilment of all His intentions
and of those of the Mother of God in regard to you.
Marvel at the dependence that the soul of the Son of
God had on His eternal Father in the ways which he
ordained for Him, and unite your soul to His. Adore
and marvel at the indissoluble unity (of the soul of Jesus)
in regard to the Divine substance, and this not alone
by subsistence, but also by actual possession, by special
assistance, and by eminent grace. . . . And ask of this
deified soul by grace and pity, a share in this indissolu-
bility so as never to depart from his ways! And if you
have devotion in seeking afresh in God this grace, since
He has occasioned in you the need of which you have
written to me; then adore the unity of the all Holy
Trinity and ask for the inseparable union by virtue of
this supreme unity."

In this quotation there are two notable things: one is the
three-fold act of the mental prayer recommended, namely
adoration, oblation and co-operation; the other is the illus-
tration the passage gives of Bérulle's distinctive idea of the
grace-giving states and conditions of our Lord's own being.

The fact that Bérulle was giving such direction to the
French province of Carmel, while in Spain their own
great doctors were being formed, now under Franciscan,
now Dominican, now Jesuit influence; and that, in
Paris itself, S. Francis de Sales' new order of the Visitation was soon to be handed over by him to the direction
of S. Vincent de Paul; and that in his direction M.
Vincent, though a disciple of Bérulle, was to show himself
far nearer in spirit and in method to S. Ignatius; the
testimonies of S. Teresa and of S. Jane Frances—all go
to show the sane eclecticism of the great teachers of that
age. A squabble of systems was the last thing they
desired; but Jansenism was soon to force on them a
conflict which was more than a squabble.

IV. METHODS OF MENTAL PRAYER OTHER THAN THOSE OF S. IGNATIUS AND SAINT-SULPICE

(DOMINICAN, FRANCISCAN, CARMELITE, SALESIAN, AND LIGUORIAN)

BY PATRICK THOMPSON

" THE great method of prayer is that there is none at all—prayer should be made by grace and not by artifice." S. Jeanne Françoise de Chantal, whose words these are, has no doubt a better right to be heard with respect in this matter than almost anyone, excepting always the incomparable S. Teresa. Nevertheless, the form in which M. Pourrat [1] reproduces her opinion is unfair to her reputation. She is speaking only of souls whom God has already raised to passive prayer, and the same dictum reproduced in its context by Canon Saudreau [2] loses much of its bluntness. "The great method of prayer is that there is none," the Saint says, " *when* the Holy Spirit has made Himself master of the person meditating, for He does what He pleases with him, and at *that* time there are neither rules nor methods. The soul must be in God's hands as clay in the hands of the potter for making all kinds of vessels, or as soft wax for receiving the imprint of the seal, or as a white tablet on which the Holy Spirit writes His divine wishes. *If,*

[1] P. Pourrat, *La Spiritualité Chrétienne*, Eng. tr.
[2] A. Saudreau, *Mystical Prayer according to St. Jeanne Françoise de Chantal*, see also *The Spiritual Life*, translated by the nuns of the Harrow Visitation.

when we go to prayer, we *could* make ourselves pure capacity to receive the Spirit of God, that would suffice for all method : prayer should be made by grace and not by artifice (that is, we should depend more on God's help than on methods)."

What it does seem fair to say is that it does not matter much which method anyone adopts. The few which have survived in general use have proved their worth by their power of survival, and comparative study of them only goes to prove that the differences between them are differences rather of attitude, of expression, and of arrangement, than of matter. The great outlines of any of them are dictated by the very contour of the human mind.

Admittedly, the Holy Spirit is the best director. Admittedly, mental prayer is simply a heart-to-heart conversation with God, and it is of the essence of good conversation to be natural. Admittedly, all doctors are agreed that the normal development of such prayer is in the sense of progressive simplification ; that the only purpose of consideration is to arouse affections, that it is, in fact, only the needle which draws after it the golden thread, or the spark which lights the fire ; that, sooner or later, the affections will normally engross the time hitherto expended on considerations, until at length they swallow up the whole ; and that the sooner this comes to pass the better.

Nevertheless, it remains true that it is, precisely, free-and-easy conversation with God which beginners find difficult ; it is precisely simplicity which seems to them monotonous and wearisome ; it is precisely the flow of spontaneous affections which they desire and are seeking to acquire. They desire to be at home with God ; they desire to find their conversation in heaven ; but they are only too painfully conscious that as yet their home is in the world, and that a dissipated life means distracted prayers; they want their prayer to help them to bring the order of virtue into their lives; and often their greatest difficulty is sheer ignorance. Therefore they want a method; they want it cut and dried; and the more cut and dried the better.

Now, many of the well-known methods were designed by religious for religious; some were conceded by religious to persons living in the world without adequate appreciation of the adjustments required by their state— all these are so far unfitted to the generality of beginners. But the generality is not the totality. There are those who, so to speak, start half-way. The immediate end in the director's view is the next stage, affective prayer, and there are souls who from the first find greater facility in acts and affections than in imagining and reasoning. Even the plea of ignorance need not necessarily keep them to a discursive method; for there is ignorance and ignorance, and what is required for success in the art of prayer, as S. Teresa recognised in her principles for the admission of novices, is not erudition, but good sense.

Methods, then, have their place, and all that is necessary is that the director should beware of making any one method into a Procrustean bed for all his penitents. The first method which must engage our attention is that of the Dominican Luis of Granada (1505–88), though its importance is rather historical than actual. It, rather than the method of S. Sulpice and the French Oratory, is to be contrasted with the Ignatian method of the three powers; these are the poles to which the mediating types are attracted and round which they group themselves. The Granadine method conditioned S. Teresa's early prayer: for she had experience of Dominican as well as of Jesuit confessors, besides learning the method directly from Luis of Granada's writings, and from San Pedro de Alcántara at second hand. It is one of the sources of the *Introduction to the Devout Life;* and the Salesian method, as method, is simply a fusion of Luis and Ignatius. It even provided the schematism for the " vulgarisation " of the high Bérullian dogmatic of devotion by MM. Olier and Tronson and S. John Eudes.

The method, expressly intended for those in the world, is to be found in the third chapter of the first part of Luis of Granada's *Libro de la Oracion y Meditacion*, appended to an arrangement of subjects for every day of the week, on the lines of the *Ejercitatorio* of Cisneros. The method, according to its author, does but " show novices the way . . . as soon as they have started on it, the Holy Spirit will teach them the rest."

It includes six parts: preparation, reading the subject, meditation, thanksgiving, offering, and petition. The subject is to be anticipated the night before, and recollected on rising. The proximate preparation, of course, involves the act of the presence of God, coloured by consideration of His incomparable majesty; which leads on to an act of humiliation for our sin, and to petition for grace. These elements would seem to be almost irreducible. They recur in some form in all methods. The offering, or oblation, so prominent later in Bérullian spirituality, comprises the offering of self and that of the merits of Christ. It provides, so to speak, a handle to the petitions which follow. Curiously enough, it is missing in the first draft of the method, in the *Libro de la Oracion*, and comes from a later work, the *Memorial de la Vida Cristiana*.

In passing, we may note that S. Francis de Sales takes both his definition of devotion, in the *Introduction*, and his distinction between meditation and contemplation, in the *Treatise on the Love of God*, almost word for word from Luis de Granada (whom he frequently cites and recommends).

The Franciscan Pedro de Alcántara (1499–1562) adopts not only the arrangement, but also the title of the Dominican writer's book, and the members of his method are precisely the same. But the treatment of them which he gives, though so warmly recommended by Fr. Bede Frost as a substitute for " rest-cures and the like," seems to be unbearably diffuse. San Pedro himself allots to the complete exercise two hours, but this is largely filled up with vocal prayers, and indeed incorporates almost all the acts and exercises which the Christian might be expected to perform in the course of the day. The preparation alone includes the Confiteor and the Veni Creator, with its versicle and collect. In the thanksgiving, after running through all the heads of the General Thanksgiving, we sum up with the Benedicite; while the description of the petition reads like an expansion of the Prayer for the Church Militant. All the methods which follow the Granadine model are, of course, lengthened by including the reading, which in the Ignatian system is generally done over-night. S. Teresa (1515–82), in her reform, at first provided for the subject of the morning's meditation, made in choir, to be given out over-night; later this was changed, and it was read immediately before the time of meditation.

No doubt it would be possible to extract a formal method of discursive meditation from S. Teresa's works; but it would not be easy: her methods of composition are anything but scholastic. Normally, however, we should go to her rather for advice on the conditions and spirit of prayer in general, and for explicit direction

F

chiefly on the prayer of recollection.[1] (With infused mystical prayer this chapter has no business.)

For the prayer practised by beginners among the discalced Carmelites, M. Tanquerey[2] (1564–1615) sends us to the Venerable John of Jesus-Mary. Fr. Bede Frost reproduces the method given in the third part of that writer's *Instruction of Novices*. It follows the familiar sexpartite division of Luis of Granada. It is expressly noted that the reading may precede the preparation. Of the meditation proper the V. John says well that it is " nothing but a discourse addressed by the intellect to the will." Again he says well of the petition following the oblation : " Have we not the right to claim that for which we have offered the price in advance? " The parts of the prayer do not differ in essence from those which we have already examined, but the incidental advice given by the author[3] is judicious and memorable. As a good Teresian, he insists on the practical primacy of the will, subordinates considerations to affections, and is at pains to remind the novices of their liberty to modify or discard the method if it fails of its end.

S. Francis de Sales (1567–1622) speaks in passing of meditation in the second chapter of the sixth book of the *Treatise on the Love of God*, and at length in the first ten chapters of the Second Part of the *Introduction to the Devout Life*. In chaps. 9–18 of the First Part himself gives examples of meditations worked out—in fact, a miniature set of Spiritual Exercises, leading up to the election of the devout life. His method is nearer to the Ignatian than to the Granadine type, comprising only the four main

---

[1] For an account of S. Teresa's teaching on Meditation, see Abbot Butler's *Ways of Christian Life*, Chap. IV., which had not appeared when this chapter was written.

[2] *Précis de Théologie Ascétique et Mystique*.

[3] See Bede Frost, *The Art of Mental Prayer*, pp. 93, 94.

divisions, Preparation, Considerations, Affections and Resolutions taken together, and Conclusion.

" I present you,"[1] he writes to Philothea, " with a short and simple method. First . . . the preparation, which consists in two points, of which the first is to put oneself in the presence of God, and the second to invoke his help. To put yourself in the presence of God I propose to you four principal means . . .

" The first takes its start from a lively and attentive apprehension of the omnipresence of God, that is to say, that God is in all and everywhere. . . . Coming then to your prayer, you must say in your heart and with all your heart: O my heart, my heart, truly God is here.

" The second means is to reflect not only that God is in the place where you are, but that He is very particularly in your heart and in the depth of your mind, which he vivifies and animates with His divine presence, being there as the heart of your heart, and the mind of your mind. In the consideration of this truth, then, you will stir up a great reverence in your heart towards God who is there so intimately present.

" The third means is to consider our Saviour who in His humanity beholds from heaven all the persons in the world, but in particular Christians, who are His children, and more specially those who are in prayer, whose actions and behaviour He observes. This is not a mere imagination, but a most true truth; for though we see Him not, yet He considers us from on high. S. Stephen saw Him thus at the time of his martyrdom; so that we can well say with the Spouse; *En ipse stat post parientum nostrum, respiciens per fenestras, prospiciens post cancellos.*[2]

" The fourth means consists in making use of simple imagination, representing to ourselves the Saviour in His sacred humanity, as if he were close to us, as we are

[1] The writer's translation.   [2] Canticles, ii. 9.

used to represent to ourselves our friends, and to say :
' I picture so and so doing this or that, I seem to see him,'
or some such thing.   But if the most holy sacrament of
the altar were present, then this presence would be real,
and not purely imaginary. . . . You will then use one
of these four means to put your soul in the presence of
God before prayer; they are not all to be employed
together, but only one at a time, and that shortly and
simply."

The second point of the preparation is the invocation.
This corresponds roughly to the Ignatian direction of
intention and prayer for the special grace desired.
" The invocation," says S. Francis, " is made thus :
your soul, perceiving herself in the presence of God,
prostrates herself with extreme reverence, recognising how
unworthy she is to remain before so sovereign a Majesty ;
and none the less, knowing that this same goodness desires it, she begs of Him the grace to reverence and serve
Him well in this meditation. . . . It will help you, too,
to add the invocation of your good angel and of the
sacred personages who are to be found in the mystery
you are meditating.   After these two ordinary points of
the meditation," continues the Saint, " there is a third
which is not common to all kinds of meditations : it is
what some call composition of place and others [in the
Granadine   scheme]   interior   reading.   This   simply
consists in proposing to one's *imagination* the body of the
mystery on which one would meditate. . . . Some will
tell you, however, that it is better to make use of the
simple thought of faith and a simple apprehension,
entirely mental and spiritual, in the presentation of these
mysteries, or perhaps to consider them as performed
within your soul; but that is too subtle for a start; and
until God calls you higher, Philothea, I advise you
to keep to the low valley to which I point you."

The second great division of the prayer is the considerations or meditation proper. For this we turn to the *Treatise on Divine Love.*[1] "We may then define this exercise," S. Francis writes, " to be a thought continued and maintained with a voluntary attention for the purpose of exciting the heart to produce holy affections, and to form salutary resolutions.

" The holy Scripture makes use of a very just comparison, (when) King Ezechias . . . says, ' I will cry like a young swallow, I will meditate like a dove.'[2]

" Young swallows open their bills very wide when they cry; and the dove, on the contrary, is the only bird which sings with its bill closed; instead of emitting its sound exteriorly, it warbles several times in its windpipe, and it is only the echo and reverberation of its notes that can be heard; its song is called cooing, and serves no less to manifest its love than to testify its grief, according to the circumstances in which it is placed. . . .

" During spring, the bee flies about and alights on every flower and blossom, not by chance, or precisely to enjoy the sight of the enamelled fields, but for the sake of seeking honey. When it has extracted the sweet liquid, it carries it to its hive, where it separates it from the wax, of which it forms the comb, and the little cells where it preserves the honey during the winter.

" The devout soul follows this plan exactly in meditation. She reflects on the mysteries of faith, not superficially, nor merely for the pleasure she derives from admiring the excellence of these wonderful objects, but to seek for holy affections, and especially for motives which may engage her to love God. . . . She then

[1] Quoted from *A New Translation* (London: Keating & Brown, 1836).
[2] Is. xxxviii. 14.

selects from the subjects of her meditation, and sets apart whatever is most calculated to procure her spiritual advancement, of which she makes the subject of the holy resolutions which are to be her support in the time of temptation."

From this excursion into natural history we return to the Introduction for the affections and resolutions, which S. Francis couples closely together. " The meditation," he continues, " diffuses good movements in the will or affective part of our soul : such are the love of God and of our neighbour, the desire of the glory of paradise, zeal for the salvation of souls, imitation of the life of our Lord, compassion, admiration, delight, fear of the displeasure of God, of judgment and of hell, hatred of sin, trust in the goodness and mercy of God, confusion for our evil life past; and in these affections the mind should dilate and expand itself as much as it can. . . .

" But you must not rest in these generalised affections, Philothea, without turning them into special and particular resolutions for your correction and amendment, thus : Well, then, I will not hereafter be offended by such and such annoying words that such and such a person, neighbour, or servant, may say of me, nor by such and such an affront put upon me by this person or that; on the contrary, I will say and do this or that to gain and soften him, and so with the rest. By this means, Philothea, you will correct your faults in a short time, where by affections alone it would cost you much time and trouble.

" Finally, you must bring the meditation to an end with three acts, made with all the humility you can muster; the first, an act of thanksgiving, thanking God for the affections and resolutions He has given us, and for the goodness and mercy we have discovered in Him in the mystery meditated. The second is an act of oblation, whereby we offer to God His same goodness and mercy, the death, the blood, the virtues of His Son, and conjointly with these, our affections and resolutions. The third act is that of supplication, whereby we beg and implore God to impart to us the graces and virtues of His Son, and to give His blessing to our affections and resolutions, so that we may faithfully put them into practice; then we pray likewise for the Church, for our pastors, relations, friends and others, using in this the intercession of our Lady, the angels and saints; finally, I have found it well to say the Pater and Ave, which is the general and necessary prayer of all the faithful."

In this fourth part, it will be noticed that S. Francis abandons the Ignatian model and simply links the three last divisions of the Granadine scheme in one. He goes on to inculcate the gathering of the spiritual nosegay. "Our mind having discoursed on some mystery by meditation, we should choose one or two points we have found more to our taste and more proper to our betterment, to call to mind during the rest of the day, and to inhale their scent. This should be done in the same place where we made the meditation, while we relax or walk up and down alone for a little while after."

In the following chapter he gives some general counsels—as that affections are never to be repressed, at whatever point they may arise; whereas the resolutions, since these deal with familiar objects, should be kept to the last, lest they prove a source of distractions.

We need make no apology for describing this method at such length in the Saint's own words, since it is probably the one most generally followed, outside " religion," after the Ignatian and Sulpician; but pass at once to the Liguorian method. We may note, in passing, that whereas S. Ignatius seeks to smooth the way for beginners by being very precise as to the form, and leaving them a wide liberty as to the content of their prayer, S. Francis pursues the same object by means of keeping down the number of his divisions, and fusing elements formerly distinguished; and S. Alphonsus by means of prescribing exactly even the considerations and affections which are to fill in the framework, recommending those which are likely to be most generally serviceable.

Another device which facilitates the learning of a method is the use of such " *aides-mémoires* " as M. Olier's " Jesus before my eyes, Jesus in my heart, Jesus in my hands." One such is to be found in Dom Chautard's searching little work *L'Ame de tout Apostolat ;* thus— Video, Sitio, Volo, Volo Tecum. A similar service is done to the Liguorian method by the writer who played Olier to the Bérulle of S. Alphonsus Mary—Père Desurmont— in that most useful handbook *La Charité Sacerdotale*, which might almost be called " Liguori without Laughter." He analyses the body of mental prayer as follows : The renewal of faith by good thoughts, the renewal of hope by good desires, the renewal of grace by prayer, and of charity by good resolutions.

The eclectic spirit of S. Alphonsus knows no scholarly scruples. Like S. Francis, he is first and last a pastor, and cares nothing whence the various elements of his teaching are derived, or whether they preserve their original integrity and proportion, so only that they be assimilable and nourishing. The flexibility of his method will be appreciated by comparing the two variant forms quoted by Fr. Frost. His originality lies rather in the emphasis with which he underlines the importance of the pervading dispositions of simple faith, utter naturalness—which is the same thing as humility—contrite love and loving contrition, and importunate prayer for perseverance.

P. Desurmont dots the i's and crosses the t's of the Salesian definition of mental prayer, which he calls " an application of (all) the faculties of the soul to the things concerning the end of man (God to glorify—God to enjoy), under the form of a conversation with heaven." All his counsels on the practice of prayer are as pregnant as they are terse; none more so than the following (quoted by Fr. Frost). First, " All prayer should be natural as to tone, without any striving after emotion, familiar and ordinary. . . . The greatest of sinners can pray provided only that he prays as a sinner; the man of evil will can and ought to pray; but *as* a man of evil will . . . the lukewarm as lukewarm, the just as just." Secondly, never fail to make use of your liberty. " Liberty to mingle vocal prayers with meditation; liberty to repeat time upon time what we wish to say to God; liberty *to adapt the acts of mental prayer to any method*, liberty to follow with discretion the inspiration of the moment or, on the contrary, *to keep to a method once for all determined* . . . liberty to descend at times, in case of need, to a lower state of prayer, or, with permission, to mount a step higher; liberty to make use of good books and to appropriate their language; liberty to meditate in an easy posture, provided it be reverent and helpful—in one word, liberty to make the work of prayer as easy as may be, provided only that it be done, and that it be done well."

Nothing is said here of Benedictine spirituality, since its characteristic contribution is rather to liturgical life than to systematic mental prayer. Ample notices of Benedictine writers will be found in Abbot Butler's *Ways*. Note especially the references to Fr. Augustine Baker's teaching on the prayer of forced acts.

PART III

DIRECTION IN PRAYER

DIRECTION IN PRAYER

By HERBERT MATHER

THE first section of this book has dealt with the theory of prayer. Prayer is the first duty and the highest privilege of the Christian soul. Therefore the first duty of the Christian priest as pastor is to acquire the science of prayer, and his highest privilege to teach the art of prayer to others. The source of this science is the revelation of the prayer of Christ and the history of the praying Church. From these sources theologians have succeeded in extracting the schema of the normal development of a prayerful soul, and various methods of procedure for it to adopt at different stages.

The most crucial stage, and that in which the director can give most help, comes at the beginning, when the believing soul first aspires to make progress, and strives to develop its prayer beyond what it learnt at its mother's knee. It is only for ordinary (discursive or affective) mental prayer that anything to be described as method is possible; we do not need a method to learn the Paternoster; we cannot hope to find a method to acquire what is by definition infused. Therefore the second section of the book has passed in review the principal methods of procedure which the Saints have bequeathed to us for this crucial stage.

Now we come to consider the general principles which should govern the director's action in imparting this science to his subjects; in fact, the pedagogy of prayer. Prayer can never be learned from charts or text-books;

for it is not merely an exercise of this power or that; it is an attitude of the whole man face to face with his Creator. That is what S. Jane Frances means when she says that "Mortification without prayer is very difficult: prayer without mortification is very dangerous." No amount of polemic in the interests of "prayer as contemplation" and "Christianity as prayer" will get rid of the stubborn facts that it is only the pure in heart who shall see God; that the heart of fallen man is anything but pure; and that it is only to be purged of its impurities by painful effort. It is the director's part to organise that effort, and so to make possible that vision.

I. The Duties of a Director of Souls

There is, then, no part of the duty of a priest more important than that of directing souls, and he should, accordingly, have a very clear idea of the scope and— may we say, also—of the limitations of his office. A director should not lord it over God's heritage, and should never be tyrannical or overbearing. After all, he is only the instrument; the work is that of God. God Himself is the true Director; the priest is merely the interpreter, showing the soul what God's will for it is. Thus, M. Olier says: "In the direction of souls we must put ourselves into the hands of our Lord as instruments which He chooses to use in order to make His will known to them, to make them walk freely in the way of perfection, to strengthen them in their weakness, to encourage them in their discouragement, to deliver them from the snares of their enemies, and to conduct them by a sure way to heaven. In order to do this we must direct them by our Lord's way, not our own; and this must be done by annihilating ourselves, in order that we may be entirely filled with the spirit of God, being intimately and inseparably united to Him, so that we may enter into the ways by which He wills to conduct souls, never directing them by our own ways, which will assuredly do great harm to them. . . . For in the Church there is but one Priest . . . one sole Director, Jesus Christ, who wills to conduct all the faithful by the ministry of His priests, and to be in all directors in order to govern all whom He has confided to them." [1]

Again, " Dame Gertrude tells us in her writing why she so much relished the instructions she received. It was because they directed all capable souls to the permanent, unchangeable Master and Teacher, who ever taught contemplative souls the same kind of doctrine, and was never in contradiction with Himself; whereas directors who do not refer the soul to the divine Master are as changeable and repugnant to one another in their instructions as they are chargeable in their office." [2]

And Père Grou says: " To direct a soul is to lead it in the ways of God; it is to teach the soul to listen for the divine inspiration, and to respond to it; it is to suggest to the soul the practice of all the virtues proper for its particular state; it is not only to preserve that soul in purity and innocence, but to make it advance towards perfection: in a word, it is to contribute as much as possibly may be in raising that soul to the degree of sanctity which God has destined for it. . . . It is necessary that the confessor should be, as it were, the voice of God, the instrument of divine grace, the co-operator with the work of the Holy Spirit, and consequently that he should be an interior man, a man of prayer, a man well versed in spiritual things, as

[1] A. de Brétonvilliers, *Esprit d'un Directeur des Âmes*, Chap. I.
[2] Fr. Augustine Baker, *The Inner Life of Dame Gertrude More*, p. 144.

much by his own experience as by study and reading; that he should have no purely natural designs, either of vanity or self-interest, but that he should only consider the glory of God and the good of souls; that he should never act according to the leadings of his own spirit, but that he should judge of the things of God by the spirit of God." [1]

The director, then, must not start out with preconceived notions of the way a soul should advance, and try to force all souls into one and the same mould. This is probably at times a snare to every director. He knows what has helped him personally in his own life, and he knows the way in which he has helped another soul to advance, and then he tries to force these methods on all souls indiscriminately. Thus Bérulle says: " To direct a soul is to direct a world which has more secrets and diversities, more perfections and rarities, than the material universe, and a more perfect relation to the archetypal world, that is, to Him who is both the creator and the idea of all that exists outside the divine essence; so that God regards a soul in a manner far different from that with which He regards the rest of creation. And we ought to honour, follow, and imitate His holy, pure and divine regard, looking upon God's work as He looks upon it." [2]

And Father Baker tells us again: " Indeed, the office of a director is not to teach a particular method to the disciple, but to give general instructions by which the soul may get into her interior, and when she has once got there, to observe the divine admonitions and guidance, instead of following the method of books, or opinions of others, custom, or what at other times has proved profitable." [3]

[1] P. J. Grou, S.J., *Manual for Interior Souls*, p. 128.
[2] Bérulle, *La Direction Spirituelle*, Chap. I.   [3] Baker, *op. cit.*, p. 73.

Again, Père Libermann tells us to recognise as a fundamental principle of direction that the person directed must not be cramped or restricted. Too many rules must not be prescribed, too rigid a system must not be followed, or harm may be done. If a director conducts and restricts his penitent overmuch, holding too closely to principles, much evil may come. In short, it is essential in direction to allow grace to act with a great freedom.

That, at least, is Father Baker's advice: "The only serious fault, indeed, which Dame Gertrude had to find with her former directors was that they had prescribed some or all of these bookish human instructions concerning mortification and prayer, without referring her for their particular application to the guidance of the Holy Spirit." [1]

Surin says the same: "There are directors who get a plan and an idea into their heads, which they think much of, and apply to all the souls that come to them, thinking that they will accomplish something great if they bring them into line with it. So they have no other object than of carrying out what they have imagined, like one who should wish all to wear the same spiritual clothes." [2]

So, too, does S. John of the Cross: "Let spiritual directors of this kind remember, that the Holy Ghost is the principal agent here, and the real guide of souls; that He never ceases to take care of them, and never neglects any means by which they might profit and draw near to God as quickly as possible, and in the best way. Let them remember that they are not the agents, but instruments only to guide souls by the rule of faith and the law of God, according to the spirit which God gives to every one. Their aim, therefore,

[1] *Op. cit.*, p. 91. [2] P. Surin, *A Spiritual Catechism*, II, iii. 2.

G

should not be to guide souls by a way of their own
suitable to their wishes, but to ascertain, if they can,
the way by which God Himself is guiding them. If
they cannot ascertain it, let them leave souls alone and
not disquiet them. Let them adapt their instructions
to the direction of God, and endeavour to lead their
penitents into greater solitude, liberty, and tranquillity,
and not fetter them when God is leading them on." [1]

The director, then, must respect the liberty of each
soul, and realise that God does not deal with every soul
in the same way. Therefore, he must be careful not
to treat all souls alike. Thus once again Father Baker
says : " From what has been said, it will be easily
understood how unfit for Dame Gertrude were the
usual instructions to be found in books about indifferent
matters; yet the right use of them belongs to the very
essence of the spiritual life. Suppose, for instance, her
director had told her to make meditation, or to use
immediate acts, or vocal prayer : none of these would
have suited her. Or if she had been able to use them
for a time, she would have to be taught when she ought
to abandon them for contemplation. But no creature
could teach her this in particular; she must seek the
guidance of the Holy Spirit and observe His light and
attractions. Or again, if a director had told her to
keep her mind actually attentive to God while engaged
in external employments, as far as they would permit,
and never to suffer any thoughts to enter her mind, or
abide there, which had not reference to God, but always
to keep her mind intent on Him, or on the humanity
of our Saviour, it would only have hindered her progress. Then for her exterior, if he had told her she
should ever be in solitude save when obedience required
otherwise; that she should always observe silence,

[1] S. John of the Cross, *The Living Flame of Love*, III. 47, pp. 87–8.

except when spoken to, or when some necessary business required her to speak, and not one word further, that she should always keep her eyes modestly cast down, and observe nothing but what obedience required; that she should refrain from conversing at the grate, or in the house, except at the call of obedience, and then converse on spiritual subjects as far as possible; that she should not listen willingly to news, though harmless in itself, for fear of distractions; that she should withdraw as much as possible from offices and employments that might cause solicitude, lest they might disturb and distract her mind; that from the very beginning of her spiritual course she should aspire to total abstraction and recollection of life—in a word, if she had been told she should lead the life of an angel on earth and make violent efforts for a speedy reformation of her nature, without taking heed of her natural inclinations, it would certainly have been destructive to both her mind and body. Yet these and similar instructions are to be found in books and in the writings of even the holiest men." [1]

Monseigneur Gay says to one of his penitents: "I shall not employ, at least habitually, in spite of your desire, the imperative formulas of which you speak. It seems to you that so you would find peace. Yes, but a natural peace, which is not what I wish. Such commands would relieve you of the burdens of life, but it is not good that you should not feel the weight of them. I will be to you as the Cyrenian, nothing more. I would help you, not substitute myself for you. Strong natures have need of obedience; weak ones, such as yours, have a gentleness which inclines to idleness. It is necessary to give to each according to their needs. I do not want you to be a slave—the word is your own

[1] *Loc. cit.*, pp. 89–90.

—a word excessive and reprehensible. I wish you to
be a son, and a son reasonable, enlightened by the
counsels of his father . . . but walking as a man, not
as a child, still less as an animal." [1]

It is obvious, then, that the director must know the
souls with whom he is dealing. Thus Libermann says
in one of his letters: " In the direction of a soul it is
necessary to begin (and this is all important) with an
understanding of its interior, supernatural state, the
state of grace and the action of grace in that soul;
seeing how far the soul is responding to its grace, to
what degree the life of our Lord, divine grace, is dominant in the soul and its works. This first consideration
is of the highest importance. If you know well the
state of a soul, the operation of God, and the action of
grace within it, you have gained a very clear knowledge of the designs of God for it. But that is not all;
the obstacles which grace finds there must also be seen,
the action of the soul and its character, the vices and
faults which exist. . . . Further, to cause a soul to
advance it must be brought back to the principle of
sanctity within it, to divine grace, that it may become
docile to it, and enabled to triumph more and more by
its power." [2]

And the director must also watch closely the response
the soul is making. Thus Joly says: " It was a favourite
saying of S. Teresa and S. Jane de Chantal that we
must never judge of a phenomenon, or the state of a
soul, or a way of life, by its beginning, but only by its
continuation and principally by its end. An impulse
may come from nature and yet rectify itself, and end
by leading us to God ; and again the impulse may be
divinely inspired and yet afterwards deviate. Man is

[1] Mgr. Gay, *Lettres de Direction Spirituelle*, Vol. IV., p. 10.
[2] Ven. P. Libermann, *Lettres*, T. III., lettre cclviii., p. 97.

responsible for the rectification through humility as for the deviation through pride, and this it is which gives its dramatic interest to the lives of the saints."[1]

II. THE DIRECTION OF SOULS IN THE PURGATIVE WAY

Having considered the priests' office as a director of souls, let us next think of the persons with whom he has to deal. Now if we take the *Interior Castle* as our guide, we shall find that many people are in the court-yard—" neither caring to enter further, nor to know who dwells in that most delightful place." More, we shall find in the First Mansion souls still very worldly, who have yet some desire to do what is right, and who think about their souls every now and then. Such we may call *believing souls*, and they have already entered on the Purgative Way. But while such will probably form the great majority of the priest's penitents, there will be also some who have made much more progress. A fair proportion of the more devout have probably got into the Second Mansion, and these are sometimes called *good Christian souls*. There will also be a few who have got into the Third Mansion, and started on the Illuminative Way, and these are generally called *devout souls :* while perhaps any priest may meet with one or two *fervent souls* nearing the end of the Illumina-tive Way in the Fourth Mansion. Those who have advanced further in the ways of perfection lie outside the limits of this study, though they are perhaps more numerous than we are accustomed to think.

Souls in the First Mansion fall, as a rule, into one of three classes:

1. *Beginners*, i.e. children who are only entering on the Christian life, and certain converts who

[1] H. Joly, *The Psychology of the Saints*, p. 98.

have but recently turned to God, and whose good dispositions are as yet but newly born.

2. *Habitués*, who have long remained in this state, and have very little desire to advance further.

3. *The Relapsed*—that is, those who once mounted higher, but have now become lukewarm or tepid.

The director has to encourage and enlighten these, to try to make them desire better things, and then lead them to see that it is possible to attain to them. For such souls, effort is the real success. They so easily think, from the bitter experience of their frequent falls, that it is no good trying. Then he must teach them what the true Christian life is:

1. A frequent intercourse with God in prayer.

2. Faithfulness in offering God all our actions.

3. A great steadfastness in removing all obstacles which would hinder us from serving Him.

4. Intimate union with God through His sacraments.

Of these, the most important is prayer. If they can be got to pray, the offering of the morning intention follows as a matter of course. The next thing to point out is that the great obstacle to their making progress is self, that " deceitful and wicked man " from whom we must pray to be delivered. For when they can be got to realise this, it is not difficult to lead them on to practices of self-denial and simple acts of mortification.

Now let us examine more closely the souls in the Second Mansion. S. Teresa tells us that in this part of the Castle are found souls who have begun to practise prayer, and who realise how important it is for them not to remain in the First Mansion. They hear our

Lord calling them to come up higher, and though they often fall into sin, yet on the whole they do respond to the call of God. Such have not yet emerged from the Purgative Way, and it is a great mistake to treat them as if they had, and apply to them rules for the more advanced. Their fight against sin is still fierce, and there must still be long conflicts before their bad natural tendencies are weakened.

As a rule, beside their ordinary prayers, such souls have recourse, willingly indeed, but without great fervour, to other practices of devotion, such as telling their beads and assisting at week-day Mass. They communicate fairly often—not that they experience great sweetness in their Communions, but they understand the greatness of the act. On the other hand, if they are easily led to practise some devotional exercise, they are equally ready to give it up on the smallest excuse. Theirs is a state of *intermittent* piety; the desire for better things comes and goes; they may experience it at Confession and Communion, or during a sermon, as S. Teresa tells us, but apart from such times desire for progress is seldom manifested. They have begun to practise self-denial; grave sins are rare, unless a specially dangerous occasion presents itself, or one in which they had, in times past, frequently fallen. They now avoid venial sins with much more care. They no longer say: "I am doing wrong; it does not matter." Yet, if self-interest or passion is aroused, they will quickly say: "It is not so very serious, after all." However, afterwards they will be really sorry for what they have done. They have the appearance of piety without true devotion; but we must be very careful not to regard them as hypocrites, for their faith is sincere in the main, and their good dispositions are real. It is on account of their inconstancy, the rapid alternations of their good and evil moments, the mixture of worldly and religious sentiments that is found in them, that such Christians do not give God's cause the constant support one might expect of them.

Such are the general characteristics of these two Mansions. There are from time to time real aspirations after spiritual progress, but virtue seems a very difficult thing to acquire, and as a rule there are still weary struggles to be endured.

According to Saudreau, there are in this Second Mansion souls who do not experience any violent assaults, but who have not got an intense longing after virtue such as is felt by more advanced souls. We notice in them the supernatural life of faith, a sincere love of the Church, and a true zeal for her interests. They are valuable auxiliaries for the priest, and only need a more complete spiritual training to make great progress in the spiritual life.

He also places in this mansion certain others: children, young men and girls, whose failings are not greatly developed, and who have been preserved from the infection of vice. If their conduct is satisfactory, they advance gradually, especially if frequent Communion holds its right place in their lives, towards the Third Mansion, which is that of true piety. Following, then, S. Teresa, we have placed in these two Mansions souls who have traversed a certain part of the way, but who have not reached a state of high perfection. Certain souls who have reached thus far fall back miserably; others remain in it without proceeding further; others rise to a much higher degree of perfection. The difference comes from the way in which they endure the trials sent to them by God.

One cause of relapse is such a trial as being deprived of the help they enjoyed and which once nourished their piety, by change of worldly circumstances, leaving their old parish, marriage, and the like. Another cause of relapse is discouragement. The director has then to remind them of what S. Francis de Sales says : " Certain falls into mortal sin do not prevent the soul from making progress in devotion, provided it has no intention of remaining immersed therein, and does not sink down into the sleep of sin."

Some remain stationary in this state without being very blameworthy. Their faith is lively, and even continues to get clearer and brighter. Their resolution to be faithful to God is sincere, but their love remains weak, and their spirit of mortification is very imperfect. Often, however, after remaining a long time in this state, they suddenly make a generous start and advance with firm steps. This is brought about sometimes by a fervent retreat, or a new friendship, or by a trial—such as a bereavement or great sorrow— borne courageously and faithfully. In circumstances such as these, grace works powerfully in souls which are already well disposed; it enlightens their minds and kindles their hearts. Then the germs of the super- natural virtues already in them grow stronger from their practice of them, and these Christians enter upon a new life of faith and piety.

How are such souls to be directed? Lallemant tells us to take an interest in them. " Be sure that you will have done more for their perfection if you have gained their hearts, than if you have given the best piece of instruction without having done so." " Let them find in you," says S. Vincent Ferrer, " a father full of com- passion for his children, who is grieved when they sin, or are slipping into grievous sickness, or are fallen into some deep pit, and does his very best to rescue them from all these dangers."

There is need, then, to be patient with them. To quote Father Baker once again: "Our Holy Father (*i.e.* S. Benedict) warns the Abbot to take heed not to break the vessel through excessive and indiscreet attempt to remove the rust. S. Benedict, therefore, condemns too much violence and haste, but would have the rust removed by gentle rubbing, little by little, lest the vessel be injured . . . moreover, our Holy Father goes on to say that the Abbot is prudently to correct and cut off the vices to which souls may be subject, as he sees may be expedient for each one. And this the Abbot does by learning and noting the internal call from God of each one, accommodating his commands thereto."[1] And to patience we have to add perseverance: "With all his loftiness of ideal, S. John did not give people up. The director will bear in mind the well-known story of the robber chief. The way to make people hopeless is to treat them as such. No one who has realised that he himself would have tried any patience except the amazing patience of Jesus, will ever dare to give up hope in another. Even if the case seem utterly hopeless, the director will cling to the penitent with earnest prayers as the mother clings to the child whose life she almost despairs of."[2]

But the kindness of a director must not degenerate into weakness. It is pleasanter and more attractive to be conciliatory; that is why we often persuade ourselves that it is wiser, for we say to ourselves that in this way we shall avoid driving away the weak, or quenching the smoking flax. Unhappily, when priests act thus, it is the Holy Spirit they are driving away, and grace that they are quenching. Direction must be practical, taking care to lay stress several times running

[1] Gen. xxxiii. 13, *op. cit.*, pp. 98-9.
[2] Sharpe, *Perfection and the Only Alternative*, pp. 26, 27.

on some specially important and practical subject; thus, at the beginning of the year, it may insist on the good employment of time; during Lent, on the practice of penance and mortification; during the month of Mary, on devotion to our Lady; during Advent on the thought of the four last things.

But because direction is to be practical, that does not mean it has simply got to be common sense, even though sanctified. Direction must be entirely supernatural, founded on the things not of man, but of God. " If any man speak," says S. Peter, " let him speak the oracles of God; if any man minister, let him do it as of the power which God giveth: that in all things God may be glorified through Jesus Christ." [1] So that: " It is necessary that Jesus Christ should do all things in the order of grace by His Spirit, as He has done all in the order of nature, and that He should be the soul and life of all things. If we speak, we should speak in and by Him, with an entire confidence in His assistance, submitting ourselves in all things to be conducted by Him alone, in order that we may act in His time and in the manner which pleases Him, according to His good pleasure and for his glory." [2] The director is made like to the guardian angels. If he is too self-confident, and remains too much attached to his own will, he imposes his own opinions upon the souls entrusted to him; he substitutes his actions for the divine action, and his judgment for the inspirations of the Holy Ghost. Thus in dealing with such souls, direction should be paternal, firm, practical and supernatural.

To come to more detail. First, with regard to *prayer*. These advancing souls still need to have recommended to them the duty of regularity and attention in their

[1] I. Pet. iv, 11.
[2] M. Olier in *Esprit d'un Directeur*, Art. I.

prayers. The director must also uphold them in times of trial. For while sufferings and trials act as an incentive to prayer in the case of fervent souls, those who are less advanced experience a feeling of great repugnance to devotional exercises in the time of trial, and begin to neglect them. So when they own that they have fallen back in their spiritual life, he must ever point out that such relapse is bound to follow whenever prayer is neglected.

He will help them, too, by getting them to assist at the daily Mass. If they wish to obtain some grace, even if it is only a temporal one, he may recommend them to make a novena during which they will hear Mass daily, or make a visit to the Blessed Sacrament, or recite the chaplet every evening. In this way he can lead them on to undertake what they had considered to be beyond their strength. Devotion to the holy souls, too, besides its intrinsic merit, has the advantage of making such Christians pray more fervently.

And, above all, in season and out of season, he must urge the duty of *mental prayer*, especially, for such souls, discursive meditation. There can be no progress that is real and lasting without this. As S. Teresa says: " Mental prayer is nothing else, in my opinion, than being on terms of friendship with God, frequently conversing in secret with him who we know loves us."

The director's duty, then, is to get his penitents to practise mental prayer. The considerations are the means, the resolutions are the end of this kind of prayer. All authors are agreed on this. All are equally agreed that for beginners a method is almost always necessary. It is only by the help of a clear practical method that masters can train their pupils. Later on, of course, the pupil comes to act more spontaneously. But though they must be urged to meditate, it is not necessary always

to use the word "meditation." Certain books have given many people an absolute horror of it. It is a help, then, sometimes, to give people a method of examination of conscience which is really a meditation, or a method of hearing Mass, or of saying the rosary, or making the Way of the Cross, or even of saying the Pater or Ave or other short prayers.

Secondly, we come to the sanctification of our common actions. Here the need is to impress the necessity of *recollection*, and of a *rule of life*. One way to inculcate recollection is to suggest short acts of the presence of God at stated times, or stated places, or again, to give frequent instruction, according to the teaching of S. Ignatius, on the use of creatures. When suggesting a rule of life, it must at first be simple and easy; it is no good having a rule one never keeps. It should embrace such things as:

1. When and how to pray, and what religious practices to adopt.

2. What virtues should be specially cultivated.

3. It should contain some counsels as to ordinary occupations and the duties of the state of life.

It is easy to get people to adopt a rule of life; it is much more difficult to get them to keep it.

Thirdly, we come to *renunciation*, which must occupy a very important place. No one can learn to pray apart from this. The director's work being to further the will of God in souls, he must never allow any considerations of human prudence to obscure the need of the use of this necessary means. He must lead souls on to realise the necessity of complete self-surrender if God is to have His own way with them. He must make them see the personal nature of religion; that religion is not a mere keeping of rules, but a burning enthusiasm for a master; the passion of the lover for the beloved. Though these souls are still only in the Purgative Way, he ought to begin to inculcate in them the loving devotion put before us by S. Ignatius in the Exercise on the Kingdom of Christ.

So the *examination of conscience* plays a very important part; and it is well to lay stress rather on the particular than on the general examen, and with such souls to suggest a virtue to be practised rather than a fault to be avoided; though of course it must bear on the dominant disposition. It is much more interesting to try to acquire something than merely to avoid something. This particular exercise is very important in simplifying the whole of the spiritual life and certainly makes the work of a director much easier.

And, in the second place, we come to two great virtues which are pre-eminently necessary—*humility* and *mortification*. Pride is the root of all sins. The director must point out the evil, encourage souls to resist it, and urge them to pray God to make them more humble. There is no sin about which people are more ignorant.

There is one more form of self-love which is very common in this state, and that is *human respect*. People will not do certain things for fear of what others will say. And if the director does not examine them on this point, they will seldom reveal this weakness. There is only one way of getting rid of fear, and that is to face it. When the bird has found out that the scarecrow is only an empty show, it is no longer frightened. If, then, souls are afraid of appearing too devout, he should urge them to make open profession of their faith, as, for example, by not saying their prayers in bed.

As regards mortification, let us remember the words

of the Imitation: " The more thou doest violence to thyself, the more progress. thou shalt make." It is sometimes a good plan in Lent to give a list of mortifications and a short explanation of their importance. At other times the director can suggest that one or other of the mortifications practised in Lent might be resumed for a week, or a fortnight.

Almsgiving is an excellent form of detachment, but here again he must be careful to explain the importance of the supernatural motive.

Then there is the importance of *passive mortification*—that is, patience or resignation. It is rare that God does not help us by providing means of mortification. He will give us trials of all sorts, through sickness, the circumstances of our lives, thwarted desires, the shortcomings of our fellow-men, misunderstandings, the sorrows of our hearts. It often seems as though it was the most important part of the work of direction to impress not only on the penitents, but also on the priest the duty and necessity of suffering if any advance is to be made. Even though another person is completely in the wrong, and has behaved disgracefully, that really should make no difference to our acceptance of suffering. The fact is, we deserve to suffer, and if we would act supernaturally, we must accept the suffering with patience and resignation.

And, lastly, as to the *use of the sacraments*, it is here safe to recommend weekly, or perhaps fortnightly, Communion as the minimum, with the aim of daily Communion in view, though perhaps the most important part to insist on is the preparation before, and the thanksgiving after Communion. The thanksgiving is as important as the preparation.

This method of direction is not so complicated as it might appear at first sight. A few well-chosen words

in the confessional after the penitent has finished his
self-accusation, *never during it*, will generally enable the
priest to give the most useful advice. Such questions
should be directed to prayer, the sanctification of
ordinary actions, what S. Ignatius called the use of
creatures, the struggle against faults, mortification and
the use of the sacraments, especially the preparation for
Confession, so as to excite deeper contrition. But the
director should avoid, as far as possible, confining himself to giving general advice which is more or less com-
monplace, but often of little value. He must enter into
the little details of life if he would be a true director
and help the souls committed to his charge to come to
the perfection to which all are called.

III. The Direction of Souls in the Illuminative Way

So far we have considered souls in the Purgative
Way; now we come to those that are in the Illuminative Way—that is, in the Third and Fourth Mansions
of the Interior Castle described by S. Teresa. Of these
Saudreau says: " By the illuminative life we mean the
condition of souls already advanced in excellence, who
easily avoid mortal sins, labour sincerely after progress,
but who are still weak with regard to venial sins, into
which they frequently fall. Having much less to fear
from the passions which may perhaps hitherto have
dominated him, the Christian now strives to fan within
his heart the flame of holy charity, and thus to become
more habituated to, and more established in, the practice
of the Christian virtues. *Proficientes ad hoc principaliter
intendunt ut in eis charitas per augmentum roburetur.*[1] " Many
souls," says Suarez, " continue all their lives in this
condition. It is, for that matter, a precious and

[1] *S.T.* 2a 2ae, 24 ad 9.

extremely meritorious state, although still far removed from perfection." The majority of ascetic books suppose that this degree of the Christian life has already been arrived at. The consolations and counsels which they contain are, in fact, addressed to such souls as are already resolved to strive after perfection; while in the states which we have previously described the wish to be saved and to lead a good Christian life indeed exists, but the desire for progress is either absent (in the first degree) or is still feeble, or only intermittently apparent." [1] And Van Acken says: " Those who are progressing on the way of perfection have better control of their passions, and hence more easily refrain from mortal sin, practise the different virtues more zealously, but do not as yet easily refrain from voluntarily venial sin, because they have not yet wholly tamed their evil inclinations. They are following the illuminative way. Grace constantly sinks deeper and deeper into their souls. They realise ever more clearly the enormity and hideousness of sin; while virtue holds greater and greater attraction for them. Their souls are filled with a longing to imitate Christ and follow in His footsteps." [2]

As a rule, the passage from the Purgative to the Illuminative Way is marked by an abundance of spiritual consolations. Some Christians, after seeming to remain stationary for a long time, suddenly appear to be strongly affected by grace. They acquire a zest for religious practices, their hearts are touched, and they become able, far better than before, to enjoy the consolations of religion. Thus S. John of the Cross says: " We are to keep in mind that a soul when seriously converted to the service of God is, in general, spiritually

[1] A. Saudreau, *Degrees of the Spiritual Life*, Vol. I., p. 128.
[2] Van Acken, *A Handbook for Sisters*, p. 13.

H

nursed and caressed, as an infant by its loving mother, who warms it in her bosom, nourishes it with her own sweet milk, feeds it with tender and delicate food, carries it in her arms, and fondles it. But as the child grows up the mother withholds her caresses, hides her breasts and anoints them with juice of bitter aloes; she carries the infant in her arms no longer, but makes it walk on the ground, so that, losing the habits of an infant, it may apply itself to greater and more substantial pursuits. The grace of God, like a loving mother, as soon as the soul is regenerated in the new fire and fervour of his service treats it in the same way; for it enables the soul without labour on its own part, to find its spiritual milk, sweet and delicious, in all the things of God, and in devotional exercises great sweetness; God giving it the breasts of His own tender love, as to a tender babe. Such souls therefore delight to spend many hours and perhaps whole nights in prayer; their pleasures are penances, their joy is fasting, and their consolations lie in the use of the sacraments and in speaking of divine things." [1]

These spiritual consolations are not unknown even in those inferior degrees of the spiritual life that we have already considered. Many, for example, experience them on the day of their first Communion, or during a procession of the Blessed Sacrament, or on a pilgrimage. At such times the emotions may be lively and consolations abundant, but apart from such occasions consolations are rare while the soul is in the Purgative Way, and as a rule they do not last very long. Such souls may, and often do, experience a sense of satisfaction at some duty fulfilled, but we have got to realise that such consolations are completely different from those of which we are now speaking, and which

[1] S. John of the Cross, *The Dark Night of the Soul*, I. i. 2 & 3, pp. 5–6.

more advanced souls experience in the ordinary exercise
of their Christian duties.

To quote Saudreau again: "The moment when this
operation of grace takes place is an important one in
the spiritual life, and it would be a serious misfortune
if the director failed to take note of its occurrence; for
he would then be unable to further it, and the effect
would be greatly impaired. It is rare, however, for
those under direction to make known their lively and
sweet emotions of their own accord. An attentive and
watchful director will nevertheless be able to recognise
them by certain signs, or, at any rate, be led to suspect
their presence; and then it will be easy for him by a
few questions to change his suspicions into a certainty.
He will perceive that a soul has suddenly become more
regular in frequenting the sacraments, more eager to
receive the Holy Eucharist, more capable of surmount-
ing obstacles which had formerly kept it away from
Communion. It will show greater assiduity to prayer
and devotional exercises, less human respect, and a
clearer and more tender conscience, while at the same
time the desire for advancement expresses itself by
obvious efforts and requests for counsel, etc. Another
sign of sensible grace is the taste which a soul discovers
for reading spiritual writings and hearing sermons.
Everything which speaks to it of God moves and
delights it." [1]

By these different marks the director ought to recognise the interior workings of the Holy Ghost, and he
will come to the conclusion that the soul has passed
from the Way of Purgation to that of Illumination.
In the Third Mansion are all those Christians who are
still either experiencing the effervescence of a budding
piety, or who, after remaining long in the state of simple
piety, have not responded sufficiently generously to the

[1] *Op. cit.*, Vol. I., p. 138.

calls of grace to merit being raised to a higher rung on the ladder of sanctity. " To return to what I began to say," says S. Teresa, " about the souls that have entered the Third Mansion. God has shown them no small favour, but a very great one, in enabling them to pass through the first difficulties. Through God's goodness I believe that there are many such in the world: they are very desirous not to offend His Majesty even by venial sins, they love penance, and spend hours in meditation, they employ their time well, exercise themselves in works of charity to their neighbours, are well ordered in their conversation and dress, and those of them who own a household govern it well. This is certainly to be desired, and there appears no reason to forbid them entrance to the last Mansions: nor will our Lord deny it them if they desire it, for this is the right disposition for receiving all his favours." [1]

The Faults of Souls at the Beginning of the Illuminative Way

Souls who have only just entered upon this life of piety cannot at first possess all the virtues in a very high degree. The natural failings of their character are more or less held in check by the action of grace, but so far they are not weakened by a sustained practice of virtue and by trials borne in a right spirit. S. John of the Cross has, in the first volume of the Dark Night, painted a picture of the imperfections of souls that are just entering on the Way of Illumination. In his enumeration of these faults he follows the order of the seven capital sins, treating them in a spiritual manner. Father Bede Frost has given a summary of this teaching in an appendix to his book on Mental Prayer. [2]

[1] The Interior Castle, Third Mansion, Chap. I., S 8, p. 43.
[2] The Art of Mental Prayer.

From the teaching of S. John of the Cross it appears that though Christian souls, when they have arrived at this point in the spiritual life, are full of excellent dispositions, they are still far from being perfect. As a matter of fact, a good many Christians spend their whole lives in this state. But while they still maintain themselves on the rung of the ladder of perfection to which they have attained, their interior condition undergoes a very great change. Sensible consolations are gradually withdrawn from them, for God, in order to effect their purification, takes them away. The sweet emotions which they formerly experienced at the thought of religious truths, or in the practice of works of piety, cease to be felt. The most striking considerations leave the heart cold. Aridity, and what perhaps we might describe as universal distaste for religion, have succeeded to the former consolations. This is the moment when a great number leave the path of prayer. This is the moment when they need a good director and perfect obedience. If they are not rightly directed, they are likely to end in one of these three conditions:

1. They may pass into a state of scruples, doubts and troubled conscience;

2. Or they may go astray and give up striving, or become negligent in prayer, and begin to seek their gratification in creatures or self-love.

3. Or their relations with God become more and more difficult. Their prayers are few and feeble. They remain divided between God and the creature, and never attain to real sanctity.

Thus S. Teresa says: " I have known some, in fact, I may say a number of souls, who have arrived at this state, and for many years lived, apparently, a regular and well-ordered life, both of body and mind. It would seem that they must have gained the mastery over this world, or at least be extremely detached from it; yet they become so disturbed and disheartened when His Majesty sends even moderate trials, as not only to astonish, but to make me anxious about them. Advice is useless; having practised virtue for so long they think themselves capable of teaching it and believe they have abundant reason to feel miserable." [1]

"Something of the same sort happens if such people meet with contempt or want of due respect. God often gives them grace to bear it well, for as He loves to see virtue upheld in public, He will not have it condemned in those that practise it, or else because these persons have served Him faithfully, and He, who is our supreme good, is exceedingly good to us all—nevertheless, these persons are disturbed, and cannot overcome, or get rid of the feeling for some time. Alas! have they not meditated on the pains of our Lord endured, or how good it is for us to suffer, and even longed to do so? They wish everyone was as good as they are, and God grant they do not think other people are to blame for their troubles and attribute merit to themselves." [2]

The Direction of Souls at the Beginning of the Illuminative Way in Recollection, Mortification and Humility.

Recollection.—As soon as the soul seems to be taking the first steps in the way of true piety, the first advice which should be given it is to keep itself recollected. The voice of God is not heard in the tumult; it is in solitude that He speaks to the hearts of men. Our tongues must be curbed; "If any man among you seem to be religious, and bridleth not his tongue, but

[1] *Op. cit.*, Chap. 2, par. 1, p. 48.   [2] *Loc. cit.*, par. 6, pp. 50, 51.

deceiveth his own heart, this man's religion is vain." [1] Nothing exposes to sin so much as dissipation. " As often as you can during the day," says S. Francis de Sales, " recall your mind into the presence of God by some one of the four methods I have mentioned: [2] consider what He is doing, and what you are doing; you will always find His eyes fixed on you with unchangeable love. Then say, O my God, why cannot I always be looking up to Thee even as Thou art ever looking down on me? Why dost Thou ever remember me, whilst I, alas! so often forget Thee? O my soul, thy true rest is in God, art thou seeking it there only? Just as the birds have their nests to which they can retreat, and the stag shelters himself in the thick forest, seeking shade and refreshment when the summer is hot; even so, Philothea, should our hearts daily seek a resting-place on Mount Calvary, or in the wounds of our blessed Lord, or in some other spot close to Him, whither to retire on all occasions, there to rest from their worldly cares, and to find protection and strength against temptation. Happy the soul which can sincerely say to the Lord, ' Thou art my house of defence, my strong tower, my shelter against the storm, and my refuge against the heat.' " [3] It is the silence of the convent that is the great safeguard of religion; and even people living in the world must use this powerful means if they are to make progress in the way of perfection. " Remember then, Philothea," says S. Francis de Sales, " frequently to retire into the solitude of your heart, even while you are externally occupied in business or society; this mental solitude need not be hindered though many persons are around you, for they do but surround your body, not your heart, which should remain alone in the presence of God. This was what King David did

[1] James i. 26. [2] Cf. Chap. VI., *supra*.
[3] *Devout Life*, Part II, Chap. XII., p. 78.

throughout his numberless cares, and we find him in the psalms perpetually exclaiming, ' My God, Thou art ever before me! The Lord is ever on my right hand. To Thee, O Lord, have I lifted up mine eyes! O Thou that dwellest in the heavens! Mine eyes are ever looking to the Lord." [1]

Recollection, then, consists in two things: in closing the heart as far as possible to the things of the world, and in opening it as widely as possible to the things of God. To quote S. Francis de Sales again: " Seek frequently to aspire after God by short but ardent efforts of your heart; admire His beauty, invoke His aid, cast yourself in spirit at the foot of the Cross, adore His goodness, often inquire of Him concerning your salvation; a thousand times a day offer your soul to Him; fix your inward eyes upon His sweetness; hold out your hand to Him as a child to his father, that He may guide you; lay Him in your breast as a fragrant bundle of myrrh, establish Him as the standard of your soul, and in every way excite your heart to the love of God, and to a tender ardent love for your heavenly spouse. It is thus that S. Augustine recommended ejaculatory prayer to the pious matron Proba: the spirit thus dwelling on the grandeur of God, and sharing an intimate communion with Him, will be perfumed with His perfections. Neither is it a difficult practice: such prayer may be interwoven with all our business and occupations without hindering them in the slightest degree; indeed, our external pursuits are rather helped than hindered by spiritual retreats and short devotions of the soul. When the traveller pauses to taste a drop of wine which will refresh and invigorate him, such a slight delay does not hinder his journey, but rather gives him new strength whereby to expedite and lighten

[1] *Loc. cit.*, p. 79.

it—he stops only that he may go forward the better." [1]

One great help to recollection is a *rule of life*. For well-disposed souls in this Third Mansion a stricter and more detailed rule is required than in the case of beginners, but great care must be taken in making it suitable to the condition and state of life of each soul. Directors often consider only the more specially religious practices of their penitents, and leave out too much the duties of their state of life. The *particular examen* on the practice of a definite virtue ought always to form an important part of such a rule.

Mortification.—" We learn even as little children," says Fr. Hollings, " that our impulses must be checked, and our wishes suppressed, and this we apprehend, if in no other way, by the punishments which come from neglecting to regulate our conduct by something more than the passing movements of desire or distaste. Thus early do we discover that which is afterwards the common experience of our life, that there are principles by which our actions must be regulated, which contradict the impulses and attractions of the moment, and that even when those impulses do not invite us to acts plainly wrong in themselves. Now this process is one which is accompanied by pain. It is good and useful to be restrained, for being what we are, and where we are, we stand much in need of discipline; but while this is certainly true, it is not an unmixed good: it involves loss of much joy in this life, for men are often restrained until they have lost heart about that which they at length can have, for " hope deferred maketh the heart sick." [2]

But P. Ravignan says: " To the greater number of

[1] *Loc. cit.*, Chap. XIII., p. 81.
[2] Hollings, *One Born of the Spirit*, p. 112.

Christian souls the word mortification has something strange and alarming about it; a something which we do not like to think about, which we are afraid to approach. That there are happy exceptions I know full well; there are pure and innocent souls who know how to regulate themselves and to mortify themselves, who bear patiently with ill-humour, bad temper, daily worry and annoyances, who seek not their own personal grati-fication and comfort, but who live by faith and walk in the path which their divine Saviour has traced for them. Yes, indeed, I know the world does present some such examples, but how rare they are! How many cowardly spirits do we find, lax with themselves, irritated by the smallest obstacle, obeying their own faulty natures, and weeping and lamenting because they find difficulty inseparable from duty and the practice of a holy life." [1]

And S. Teresa says of mortification and humility: " O sovereign virtues! Rulers of all created things; queens of the world; our deliverers from all the snares and traps of the devil, dearly loved as you were by our teacher, Jesus Christ, who never for a moment lived without you! Those who possess you may sally forth and fight with all hell and the whole world and its temptations! Let them not be afraid, for theirs is the kingdom of heaven; they have no cause for dread, for they care not if all be lost—nor do they count it loss—their sole fear is lest they should offend their God; they implore Him to preserve these virtues in their souls lest by their own fault they should lose them. It is true that these virtues have the property of hiding themselves from their owner's sight, so that he never believes he possesses them, whatever he may be told to the contrary. Yet he esteems them so highly that he is always striving to gain them, and thus grows more perfect in them.

[1] P. Ravignan, *Spiritual Conferences*, pp. 5, 6.

The possessor of these virtues soon unwittingly reveals them to those that talk to him. But what presumption for me to praise humility and mortification, which have been so extolled by the King of glory, and exemplified by all His toils and sufferings! These are the virtues you must labour to obtain in order to escape from the land of Egypt. My daughters, when you possess them, you will find the manna! then all things will taste sweet to you; however bitter the world will find them, to you they will be delicious." [1]

So speaks S. Teresa, and all the saints with her. Even to reach this Third Mansion it was necessary to do some violence to oneself, to struggle against self and to conquer it in many ways. " The essential state of the soul," says Fr. Hollings, " and therefore its capacity for a life of prayer is, then, let us repeat, conditioned by the way in which the faculties of our life are being exercised: for instance, we cannot wilfully use or misuse our memory, we cannot restrain or neglect to regulate its movements, without affecting our very life, for it is not only true that there is an order in our life, but also that that order is not of dissevered elements, but of wonderfully intimate adherences and interdependence of parts. As in a kingdom one element of disorder may bring all estates to ruin, so in the kingdom of the soul there can be nothing in disorder, but it must affect every part of our life, and thus the substantive estate of our soul before God is the result of all the acts of our life, and so is open before Him who knoweth the counsels of the heart, which counsels one day he shall ' make manifest ' to all." [2]

But in order to keep ourselves from slipping back, and still more if we are to make progress in the way of

[1] S. Teresa de Jesus, *The Way of Perfection*, Chap. 10, pars. 3, 4, p. 65.
[2] *Op. cit.*, p. 135.

perfection, we must needs continue this warfare on self
and apply ourselves earnestly to mortification. It is
easy enough to practise when the soul is full of consolations; but all too hard to persuade those whose progress
seems to be arrested of their need of mortification.
" Mortification in the Catholic sense," says Abbot
Vonier, " is essentially the asserting of the body, not
its negation. The aim of mortification is to strengthen
virtue. The Church never took any other view of mortification. Now virtue is in the senses; it is the highest
perfection of the senses; it is purity and strength of
character. Mortification is to mortify, or to deaden,
not the senses, but those unruly appetites that weaken
the sense of purity, that weaken the moral fibre of a
man. To make a man pure and to make a man strong,
such is the aim of mortification. To repress anything,
to abstain from anything, without that end in view, is
not a virtuous act, but an unwise act, an imprudent act,
an act that is against reason." [1]

The director ought to study carefully the rules given
by S. Ignatius in the Additions to the First Week of the
Spiritual Exercises; though, as a rule, it is not wise to
put them, as they stand, into the hands of penitents.
They must be taught, also, the great need of patience
in *passive mortification*. " My instructions to Dame
Gertrude," says Fr. Baker, " on the subject of mortification may be embraced under three heads. First,
that she should do all that belonged to her to do by any
law, human or divine. In this was comprised obedience
to divine inspirations, not only in matters of obligation,
but also in things that were indifferent; for divine
inspirations are to be observed by spiritual persons as a
law of prime importance. Secondly, that she was to
refrain from those things that were forbidden her by

[1] A. Vonier, O.S.B., *The Human Soul*, pp. 127–8.

human or divine law, or by divine inspirations. Thirdly, that she should bear with as much patience and resignation as possible all crosses and contradictions to her natural will which were inflicted by the hand of God. Such, for instance, were aridities, temptations, afflictions, or bodily pain, sickness and infirmity; or again, loss of honour or esteem, unkindness or neglect; or again, the loss of friends or want of necessaries or comforts. All this was to be endured patiently, whether the crosses came directly from God, or by means of his creatures. These, indeed, were mortifications enough for Dame Gertrude, or for any other soul." [1]

Humility

Dubly, in his *Life of Cardinal Mercier* (pp. 116–117) tells us: "Humility is not that kind of puerile, forced, and (at bottom) hypocritical convention, which constrains a man to the practice of an assumed ignorance of the divine liberality of which he is the recipient, and to an apparent abdication of himself from shyness, or a false attitude. It consists in loyalty to truth and a right balance in the moral order, because by putting man in his proper place it regulates his thoughts and affections in the sight of God, both as concerning himself and others. From this happy mingling of influences results the perfect man, a man gifted in a rare degree with that quality considered by S. Thomas Aquinas as the master quality in men fitted to govern—the *discretio rationis*, the sense of due proportion."

The humility needed by souls in the Third Mansion is not the ordinary humility of general precept. There is a more perfect humility which supposes a more delicate knowledge than that possessed by the rank and file. " The practices of humility," says Tissot,

[1] A. Baker, O.S.B., *op. cit.*, pp. 96–7.

" ought to liberate the mind, just as the practices of self-denial ought to liberate the heart, and as the practices of mortification ought to liberate the senses. My mind is made to see God and I am always looking at myself. Humility comes to correct my vision. And the first thing that humility tells me is that I have nothing of myself. It does not say that I have nothing at all, but that I have nothing through myself. I do not exist of myself, and nothing that I have comes of myself. Neither my existence nor any of the gifts of existence in me is through myself. What I have of myself is nothing. Through myself I get sin, the tendency to evil, weakness, imperfection, and all the miseries, the witness of which I bear in myself. And humility, which is truth, makes me see and recognise the nothingness which I am of myself. It does not frown at the lessons of its own nothingness, which are given to man in so many experiences and in so many shapes. To acknowledge one's sins and mistakes, not to persist in one's own views, to admit one's imperfections and shortcomings, to accept inward and outward humiliations, to draw conclusions preferably against oneself and in favour of others, this is what is suggested by humility." [1]

This humility was unknown to pagan philosophy, and is above the powers of nature. Our Lord said to S. Catherine of Siena; " Knowest thou what thou art, and art not, and who I am? If thou knowest these two things thou shalt be blessed. Thou art who art not, and I am who am. If thou hast this knowledge in thy soul, the enemy shall never deceive thee, and thou shalt escape all his snares; thou wilt never do anything against my commandments and wilt obtain every grace, every truth, every enlightenment." [2]

[1] Tissot, *The Interior Life*, p. 276.
[2] *La Vita di Sa. Caterina de Siena del Beato Raimondo.*

The director's first care, then, must be to inculcate in his penitents the principles of humility, by making them frequently dwell on them, so that they may be as convinced of them as they are now of the first truths of religion. S. Paul expresses it: " For who maketh thee to differ from another? And what hast thou that thou didst not receive? Now if thou didst receive it, why dost thou glory, as if thou hadst not received it? " [1] And these are the three stages of the practice of humility:

1. To admit our own shortcomings.
2. To be content that others should recognise them.
3. To accept humiliations.[2]

The Prayer of Souls at the Beginning of the Illuminative Way :

(*a*) The kind of prayer most suitable for souls in the Illuminative Way is that commonly called Affective. There is no need to describe that kind of prayer. We refer here only to some of the difficulties encountered in the practice of it. Often, as S. Francis de Sales tells us, the soul engaged in this kind of prayer will be deprived of all sentiments of devotion to such an extent that she seems to be in a desert land in which there is neither track nor way that leads to God. As to the causes of these drynesses or aridities, Libermann says: " These drynesses or aridities arise sometimes from some unfaithfulness, some seeking after or delight in a creature. Souls in such aridity must be gently treated: they should be obliged to make an examination of themselves and form resolutions upon it, that they may be established in feelings of self-humiliation before God. We

[1] I. Cor. iv. 7.
[2] Cf. Olier, *Catéchisme Chrétien*, quoted in Tanquerey, *op. cit.*, pp. 714–15.

must console them, and give them peace, as far as
possible, by rendering them submissive to the will of
God and obedient to His good pleasure.   Sometimes this
state is not a consequence of any fault, but God is
anxious to try their humility and gentle submission to
His divine will, and their fidelity in the midst of dryness.
The director should take advantage of these moments
to detach them and show them that sensible consolations
are by no means all-important, but that they are rather
nothing at all, and often only result in our becoming too
attached to them; that it is necessary for them to give
themselves up entirely to God, for perfection consists in
this: that they must make use of all graces in order to
be more truly His, and not think themselves more holy
because of the greater abundance of their sentiments.
They will be more capable of understanding these
considerations at such a time than when they are
abounding in joys." [1]

"Souls in a state of aridity," says Saudreau, "must
then be reminded that grace is not to be felt, that it may
exist in the soul unknown to us, and that sensible impressions and emotions, consequently, are not grace, but are
given to us on account of our weakness, to encourage us
to pray, just as people give children jam, which has
hardly any nourishment, in order that they may eat
the bread, which is a more substantial food; that
fidelity in times of dryness is much more conducive to
the soul's progress than prayers which are full of the
most sweet consolations, because it is the occasion of
more steadfast and ardent acts of love." [2]

Again, there are persons who acquiesce so easily in a
state of dryness that they scarcely struggle at all against
distractions.   Such souls must be encouraged to strive

[1] Ven. P. Libermann, *Spiritual Writings*, p. 166 (adapted).
[2] *Op. cit.*, Vol. I., p. 270.

against vain thoughts, to make acts of humility, to kiss the crucifix, and make repeated acts of love. S. Francis de Sales says: " Do not be disheartened, however great your dryness, only continue to present yourself devoutly before God. How many courtiers daily appear before their sovereign without a hope of speaking to him, content to be seen by him, and offer their homage? So, Philothea, must we pray, purely and simply, in order to do homage to God and show our faithfulness. If it pleases His divine Majesty to speak with us, to hold converse with us by His holy inspirations and inward consolations, it is doubtless a great honour and unspeakable delight; but if He vouchsafes not so to favour us, neither speaking nor even appearing to perceive us, as though we were not in His presence; yet we must not therefore quit it; on the contrary, we must remain devoutly and meekly before His sovereign goodness, and then He will assuredly accept our patience, and observe our assiduity and perseverance; so that when we again come before Him, He will look favourably on us, and reward us with His consolations, bidding us taste the sweetness of devout prayer." [1]

(b) Again, those in aridity must be taught that they will never taste the joys of prayer, or draw any benefit from it unless they apply themselves simultaneously to the practice of mortification. S. Bernard, speaking of those imperfect religious who do not share in the consolations of their more fervent brethren, explains the cause thus: " They seek to procure miserable consolations for their carnal nature by words, actions or other means. If for a time they deprive themselves of these, they never entirely renounce them. So . . . their compunction is not continual; it only lasts a few hours —what do I say?—a few instants. A soul which is a

---

[1] *Devout Life*, Pt. II., Chap. ix., p. 73.

I

slave to these pre-occupations cannot be satisfied by the visits of the Lord. *Impleri visitationibus Domini anima non potest quae his distractionibus subjacet.* The more it is able to empty itself of the first, the more it will be filled with the second. If it empties itself generously it will be abundantly filled: it will receive little if it empties itself little." [1]

Again, S. Vincent de Paul says: " Mortification is another means, my daughters, which will be a great help to you when you begin to pray. Prayer and mortification are two sisters who are so closely united together that one will never be found without the other. Mortification goes first and prayer follows after, so that, my dear daughters, if you wish to become daughters of prayer as you should, learn to mortify yourselves; mortify the external senses, the passions, the judgment, the will, and do not doubt but that in a little while by keeping to this road, you will make great progress in prayer. God will take care of you; He will regard the humility of his handmaidens, for mortification springs from humility." [2]

Mortification and prayer, says S. Jane Frances,[3] are the two wings of a dove on which we may fly away into some holy retreat, and find our rest in God, far from the tumult of men. Birds cannot soar aloft with one wing only, so we must not think that with mortification alone and without prayer the soul can take flight, that it may rise to God. Mortification without prayer is labour lost; prayer without mortification is like meat without salt—it easily corrupts. We needs must, then, give our souls these two wings on which to take flight to

[1] S. Bernard of Clairvaux, Sermon for the Ascension, No. 7.
[2] Conference 37 on Prayer, quoted in *S. Vincent de Paul and Mental Prayer*, p. 151.
[3] See *Mystical Prayer according to S. Jane Frances de Chantal*, by A. Saudreau.

the heavenly court where we shall find the full satisfaction of our hearts in conversation with our God.

IV. The Direction of Fervent Souls

So far we have considered souls at the beginning of the Illuminative Way; now let us think of those who have advanced, are nearing its end, and have already reached the state of fervour. Fervent souls differ from the merely pious in so far as they understand better and practise more completely the renunciation demanded of them. Thus Lallemant says: " We spend whole years, and often a whole life, in bargaining whether we shall give ourselves wholly to God. We cannot make up our minds to so complete a sacrifice. We reserve to ourselves many affections, designs, desires, hopes, pretensions, of which we are unwilling to strip ourselves in order to put ourselves in that perfect nudity of spirit which disposes us to be fully possessed by God. These are so many ties by which the enemy holds us bound, that he may prevent our advancing in perfection. We shall be sensible of the cheat at the hour of death, when we shall see that we have let ourselves be amused by trifles, like children. We fight against God for whole years, and resist the movements of His grace, which urge us interiorly to rid ourselves of a part of our miseries, by forsaking the vain amusements which stop our course, and giving ourselves to Him without reserve and without delay. But burdened with our self-love, blinded by our ignorance, deterred by vain apprehensions, we dare not take the step; and for fear of being miserable, we continue in our misery, instead of giving ourselves fully to God, who desires to possess us only to set us free from our miseries. We must renounce, then, once for all, all our own interests and all our own satisfactions, all our own designs, and all our own choices, that we may henceforth be dependent only on the good pleasure of God, and resign ourselves entirely into His hands." [1]

Not that mortification or renunciation is ever an end in itself; it is merely the means towards that perfect union with God in charity which is the end and aim of the Christian. Fervent souls, then, have the virtue of charity in a high stage of development. S. Bernard says: " At first man loves himself for his own sake, for he is carnal-minded and takes pleasure in nothing but himself. When he perceives that he cannot exist by and through himself, he begins to seek and love God as indispensable to his own existence. In this second stage he loves God, but for his own sake, not God's. When, however, impelled by his own need, he has begun to honour God and to occupy his mind with Him in meditation, reading, prayer and obedience, he gradually learns to know Him better, and to love Him more ardently. And when once he has tasted how sweet the Lord is, he enters upon the third stage of charity, i.e. he loves God no longer for his own sake, but for God's sake. In this stage he presumably remains, and I do not know whether any man ever attains the fourth stage in which God is loved solely for His own sake. Let those that have experience tell us of it; I for one regard this stage as unattainable here, though it will undoubtedly be the portion of the good and faithful servant when he enters into the joy of the Lord, and becomes inebriated with the fullness of the house of God." [2] A modern writer says the same: " The servant looks only to the commandments: what must be done and what must be avoided. In effect he says: ' If the Lord will not be desperately angry with me I shall omit this duty or indulge

[1] P. Louis Lallemant, S.J., Spiritual Teaching, p. 38.
[2] S. Bernard of Clairvaux, Epist. XI., No. 6.

that passion.' He is ruled by the fear of the Lord, and
' the fear of the Lord is ' only ' the beginning of wisdom ';
the consummation of wisdom is Love, for ' perfect love
casteth out fear.' No wonder to the eyes of the servant
the world and all that happens in it seems so hard to
understand. For over and over again there are happen-
ings that are only understandable to the eyes of Love.
Fear brings no light and no solution of their mystery.
For years we have striven and toiled and spent our
strength to build up a work for God, and He takes it
and smashes it: to the servant it is so crushing and
overwhelming that he is cast into the depths of despair.
He feels all is lost, that God has cast him off and dis-
owned him. Often such a one becomes embittered
against God and against the human instruments God has
used in bringing about the seeming failure. The more
he reflects on the particular happening, the more
incomprehensible it appears, the more he looks at the
human instruments, the more embittered he becomes
against them. Oftentimes the rest of the life of such a
one is clouded and shadowed by a sense of grievance
against God and man. Again, to how many is religion
only a hard round of grinding service to a God who
exacts the last farthing without one ray of love to warm
the chill round of daily duty. Now, the soul of the
lover sees all things from her Lover's point of view.
Love transforms all it touches: from the first moment
when Love awakens and quickens the soul she is quiver-
ing with the thrill of her new life: the whole world has
changed, for she has heard her Lover saying: ' Behold
I make all things new.' To the lover the ways and acts
of Love are always delightful, always pleasing. To the
soul in love everything her Lover does is well: she knows
that He who acts is infinite in Love as well as in Power:
He is not merely one who knows with absolute certitude

everything that shall befall her, but one whose Love is as absolute as His certitude, and whose every act permissive and absolute is ruled by that Love. If Love takes and smashes the slowly built-up gift of years of toil, all is well, because whatever infinite Love does must be well. The lover rejoices in the will of her Lover, cares nothing for herself, has no thought for self, but only for Him. If He is pleased, nothing else matters. She lives for the good pleasure of His will, she would not change one single happening, even although she might give as much glory if it should be changed to meet her own desire; she would rather suffer and be crucified that His good pleasure might be satisfied. To the soul of the lover, pain becomes pleasure; she would not be free from suffering, for, after all, it is suffering that likens her to her Lover. She would share all His wounds and suffer all the bitterness of His cross. Her Lover was thorn-crowned and lifted up, a red figure, dripping blood on the gibbet of the cross; how can she rejoice save in being made like Him? There is the great contrast between these two states, the one running and rejoicing in suffering and crucifixion, the other complaining, rebelling, and finding the way of the cross harsh and cruel." [1]

And Fr. Hollings tells us: "Yes, 'Love is the fulfilling of the law' here, as in what concerns all the commandments, but love is life and joy, for God our life is love and joy, and as we have 'the love of God shed abroad in our hearts,' we shall increasingly advance towards the perfect union of our being with His, and shall be saved from sinking down into the dying life of an idolatrous service; idolatrous, because although the vision of God, upon which it was once based, was a true revelation, it had become to us a lie and a snare, because

[1] Williamson, *The Triumph of Love*, pp. 20–22.

we would not embrace that of which He knew us to be capable, and so the light which was in us has become but darkness. But let us rather cry to Him, out of the deep of that self-abasement which must accompany any real approach to God, for so ' one deep calleth another,' the deep of our nothingness to the deep of God's tender mercy and fathomless love, and He shall hear and bless and quicken us." [1]

Not that these fervent souls are already perfect, though to the outward eye they may sometimes seem to be so. Such was the teaching of Suso. In one of his visions our Lord told him: " They are dear to me, but they are not yet perfect; the devil deceives them by his wiles, they fall into his snares through performing their actions with complacency and self-will. Although they are far advanced in my grace and friendship, the lack of detachment in their own will deprives them of those particular and secret favours which I grant to my well-beloved, and because of the imperfection which is in them, they will have to be purified in the flames of purgatory, and will have a lower place in heaven than my intimate friends."

S. Teresa urges those who have reached this state to avoid most carefully all occasions of offending God. The soul is not yet fully established in virtue, but is like a newborn babe first feeding at his mother's breast; if he leave her, what can he do but die?

So though the fervent soul has many and excellent dispositions, it still, too, has many failings, for though it has an ardent desire for perfection, and realises its need for complete humility and self-surrender, yet its renunciation is still imperfect.

[1] *Op. cit.*, p. 126.

The Progress of a Fervent Soul

Souls reach the stage of fervour through ardently desiring suffering. " Action is necessary," says Joly, " to the saints on account of their desire for suffering and also on account of the kind of suffering they desire. They have no love of passive suffering or sadness, and they cannot find words enough in which to condemn it. . . . The saints, therefore, love active sufferings, or, to use their own words, the pangs of travail. For a single soul, for a city or a country, for an institution which hatred would endeavour to suppress, for an Order which is to be laborious, banned and charitable, for a church, they rejoice to feel those pangs of spiritual childbirth, and in the language of all the mystics, such childbearing is the fruit and token of love." [1]

" Those who come to [Christ] as the good physician," says Fr. Hollings, " must be ready to submit to such exercises and restraints as belong to the processes of his healing art. We may have to pass through deeper sorrows, more searching pains, on the way to a true and perfect healing, but we must just trust to Him and not be surprised, but patient. Do we not, indeed, experience this in natural things? For example—one who would have his eyesight healed of a cataract must consent to lose his sight altogether for awhile; when, however, the light is again admitted to his chamber, it is to lighten eyes once impaired, but now made whole. Moreover, since throughout our life on earth we are liable to a disease which affects every faculty of our life, the disease of sin,—we must be ready to submit every faculty of body, soul and spirit, to the obedience of Christ, to be chastened by Him, to die to all for Him, that,

[1] *Op. cit.*, p. 173.

being healed, we may become the instruments of the divine glory." [1]

This desire for suffering comes very largely from prayer, for the lights which come to such souls during their affective prayer will show them little by little the necessity of dying to themselves in order that they may live for God alone. And besides all this, God often leads pious souls to this disposition of fervour by allowing them to be assailed by violent temptations. "The divine perfections," says Marimion, "exact that every rational free creature should be subjected to trial before being admitted to enjoy future beatitude. It is needful that, standing in God's sight, this creature should be placed in the face of trial and should freely renounce all satisfaction of self in order to acknowledge God's sovereignty and to obey His law. God's sanctity and judgment demand this homage. This choice, glorious for the infinite being, is for us the foundation of that merit which the Lord rewards with heavenly beatitude. . . . Eternal life will be our recompense because, having had to choose, we resisted temptation in order to cleave to God; undergoing trial, we remained faithful to the divine will. Gold is tried in the furnace; constancy in the midst of temptation reveals a soul worthy of God. Such is the condition of every free creature." [2]

As the soul advances there comes a transformation in the operation of grace; the sensibility grows fainter and the old motives for serving God no longer have the same powerful effect. Fervour of will takes the place of sensible fervour. Usually this crisis causes great suffering. "At this time," says S. John of the Cross, "God leaves them in darkness so great that they know not

---

[1] *Op. cit.*, p. 62.
[2] D. Columba Marmion, O.S.B., Abbot of Marédsous, *Le Christ dans ses Mystères*, p. 220.

whither to betake themselves with their imaginations and reflections of sense. They cannot advance a single step in meditation, as before, the inward sense now being overwhelmed in this night, and abandoned to dryness so great that they have no more joy or sweetness in their spiritual exercises, as they had before; and in their place they find nothing but insipidity and bitterness. For, as I said before, God now, looking upon them as somewhat grown in grace, weans them from the breasts that they may become strong, and cast their swaddling-clothes aside: He carries them in His arms no longer, and shows them how to walk alone. All this is strange to them, for all things seem to go against them." [1] This crisis is usually called the night of the senses.

" The great secret of God's conduct with regard to the soul which He desires to sanctify," says P. Grou, " is to take from it every kind of confidence in itself, and to abandon it to its misery. To this end, He has only to withdraw His sensible grace, to leave the soul to itself, to expose it to the lightest temptation. Soon it begins to feel distaste and repugnance; it sees obstacles and difficulties everywhere; it succumbs on the least occasions; a look, a gesture, a word disconcert it—this same soul which considered itself impervious to the greatest dangers. It flies to the opposite extremity; it is afraid of everything; it is discouraged, thinks that it will never be able to conquer itself in anything; it is tempted to give up everything. And indeed, it would do so if God did not quickly come to the rescue. God continues these dealings with the soul until by repeated experiences He has quite convinced it of its nothingness, of its incapacity, for all good, and of the necessity of resting only upon Him. This is the purpose of the

[1] S. John of the Cross, *The Dark Night of the Soul*, pp. 32–3.

temptations to which it sees itself ready to succumb a hundred times, and in which God upholds it when all hope seems to be lost; the revolt of passions which it thought to be extinct, and which now reassert their sway with such violence that the reason is obscured and the soul stands within a hair's-breadth of destruction; faults of weakness of every kind into which God purposely allows the soul to fall in order to humble it; disgusts, strange difficulties in the practice of the virtues, great repugnance to prayer, and the other exercises of piety— in a word, the profound and lively consciousness of the malignity of nature and its hatred for everything good. God employs all these means in order to annihilate the soul in its own eyes, to fill it with hatred and horror of itself, to convince it that there is no crime, however terrible, of which it is not capable—not the least good action, not the least effort, not the least desire, nor the least good thought, which it is able to produce of itself." [1]

This suffering that the soul has to undergo is indeed the work of God. He desires to strengthen the soul by removing all the attractions of the senses and to oblige it to enter on the state of pure faith. As de Besse says: " The heart is absolutely dry. Far from experiencing sweet, delightful emotions which direct it towards God, it more often feels only aversion and disgust. David had passed through this state when he said: ' In the sanctuary have I come before Thee, to see Thy power and Thy glory, and now I am in a desert land where there is no way and no water.' But the will, on the other hand, is strongly attracted towards God. It feels the need of Him; it has no peace except in adhering to Him. Thus did David rest even in the desert sanctuary. He confessed his utter dulness of intellect, which made him feel like an animal and then adds: ' *Et ego semper tecum ;*

[1] P. Grou, *A Manual of Interior Souls*, p. 89.

And I am always with thee. I do not wish to depart from thee under the pretext of having nothing to say.' This paralysis of mind and heart is only in regard to God. The soul is absolutely unable to frame any good thought or sentiment to help the will to pray. But the heart and mind are by no means powerless with regard to creatures. On the contrary, the imagination often runs at random, and the senses feel attracted to earthly things; the will alone is drawn towards God." [1]

Over and above their sensible fervour, these souls retain an acquired fervour which resides in the will and enables them to practise acts of renunciation and self-surrender without any inclination or attraction. S. Ignatius lays stress on the importance of indifference in order to attain this state of fervour.

" But how long," says S. John of the Cross, " the soul will continue in this fast and penance of sense, cannot with certainty be told, because it is not the same in all, neither are all subjected to the same temptations. These trials are measured by the divine will, and are proportioned to the imperfections, many or few, to be purged away ; and also to the degree of union in love to which God intends to raise the soul: that is the measure of its humiliations, both in their intensity and duration. Those who are strong and more able to bear suffering, are purified in more intense trials, and in less time. But those who are weak are purified very slowly, with weak temptations, and the night of their purgation is long; their senses are refreshed from time to time lest they should fall away; these, however, come late to the pureness of their perfection in this life, and some of them never. These persons are not clearly in the purgative night, nor clearly out of it; for though they make no progress, yet in order that they may be humble and know

[1] Ludovic de Besse, *The Science of Prayer*, p. 39.

themselves, God tries them for a season in aridities and temptations, and visits them with His consolations at intervals lest they should become faint-hearted, and seek for comfort in the ways of the world. From other souls, still weaker, God, as it were, hides Himself that He may try them in His love, for without this hiding of His face from them they would never learn how to approach Him. But those souls that are to enter so blessed and high a state as this of the union of love, however quickly God may lead them, tarry long, in general, amidst aridities, as we see by experience." [1]

S. Teresa laments the same fact: " God shows, by bestowing these pledges on the soul, that He designs it for great things. The fault will be its own if it does not make great progress. However, if He sees that, after He has set within it the kingdom of heaven, it returns to this world, not only will He desist from revealing to it the mysteries of His kingdom, but He will only show it the former favour at rare intervals and for a short time. I may be mistaken, but I have both seen and known that this occurs. I believe that the reason why so many persons fail to become thoroughly spiritual is that they do not worthily respond, by their actions, to this signal grace by preparing themselves to receive it again. They withdraw from our Lord's hands their will, which He considered His property: as they centre their affections on base things, He seeks other souls whose love for Him is so fervent that He can grant them even more sublime favours. Still, He does not altogether deprive the former persons of what He gave them, provided they keep a good conscience." [2]

[1] *Op. cit.*, Bk. I., Chap. XIV., pp. 66–7.
[2] *The Way of Perfection*, Chap. XXI., pp. 205, 206.

The Direction of a Fervent Soul

" As a soul," says Fr. Longridge, " perseveres in the prayer of acts or affections, her exercise will tend to become simpler and more uniform in character. At first her acts will probably be many in number and various in kind, and there will still be a certain limited use of the understanding and the imagination in making them. The soul still needs to strengthen her acts and affections by brief considerations or images in order to prolong their virtue and deepen their impression. Gradually, however, the acts and affections become stronger and independent of this help, because they become more spiritual, more purely acts of the naked will. At the same time, they become simpler and fewer in number, because each lasts longer. Whereas at first the soul made use of a number and variety of acts and affections, such as humility, contrition, faith, hope, love, adoration, resignation, etc., now many of these acts no longer correspond to her present state, nor is she attracted to them. There is a tendency for a few, and often for a single one, to become predominant. Not that it is continuous to the exclusion of all others, but it returns again and again of its own accord. This constant recurrence of one principal thought or affection, and a corresponding attraction to it, point to an increased action on the part of God. The soul has not yet entered upon extraordinary or passive prayer, but it may be approaching it." [1]

The director, then, must teach the soul to learn to delight in the repose of love as soon as it manifests itself, and persuade it that its prayer has been excellent when it has maintained itself in God's presence without even having entertained any distinct thoughts or really ardent

[1] W. H. Longridge, S.S.J.E., *Retreats for Priests*, p. 335.

affections. The soul will need great encouragement when its prayer changes. S. Francis de Sales says: " You also wish to know if a soul, still very imperfect, can with profit to itself remain in prayer before God with that simple attention to His divine presence of which I spoke. I tell you that if God places you there, you can certainly remain there, for it happens not infrequently that our Lord gives this repose and tranquillity to souls which are not thoroughly purged. While, however, they still need purgation, they should, outside the time of prayer, occupy themselves with the reflections and considerations necessary for their amendment. Indeed, even if God should keep them always in deep recollection, they still retain sufficient liberty to discourse with the understanding on many indifferent subjects; why, then, should they not be able to ponder and form the resolution needed for their amendment and the practice of virtues? " [1]

Thus the director must help fervent souls to be recollected, prayerful and humble. " We often remark," says Mrs. Herman, " about an individual that he would be such a beautiful character, if only he added humility to all his other virtues; as it is, the effect of his personality is marred by the lack of that crowning grace. But humility is not something that may be superadded to a character in order to give it an attractive ' finish.' . . . It is not something that can be done without at a pinch, but which, if added, makes a vast improvement. On the contrary, it is the framework of true manhood, the keystone of the arch of Christian character. Were it merely equivalent to ' modesty,' freedom from boasting and vulgar self-assertion, it could be treated as a surface dressing of the soul—a matter of ' good form ' rather than an essential of right being. But it is fundamental and

[1] S. Francis de Sales, *Spiritual Conferences*, No. II., pp. 26–7.

indispensable, because it is founded upon a deep and abiding sense of God. To be humble is to see ourselves, not as others see us, but as God sees us, and therefore as we are. It is, in the last resort, to adjust ourselves to God, to find our true level in the world of reality. But such self-adjustment is not a crushing, unnerving process. It is a laying hold upon the very strength of the universe, a realisation of our true dignity, our royal destiny. Manhood at its highest is nothing else but a response of the whole personality to God, a resolute and free acceptance of His standard of values, His purposes and intentions, His mind and will for the whole of life." [1]

S. Teresa continually emphasises the importance of humility. " Practice, then," she says, " what I advised in the preceding mansions, humility, humility ! For God lets Himself be vanquished by this and grants us all that we ask. The first proof that you possess humility is that you neither think you now deserve these graces and consolations from God, nor that you ever will as long as you live. . . . If we are really humble and annihilate ourselves, not only in imagination (which often deceives us), but if we truly detach ourselves from all things, our Lord will not only grant us these favours, but many others that we do not know even how to wish for. May He be for ever praised and blessed." [2]

" The root of humility," says Lallemant, " is the knowledge of God: for it is impossible to know and feel our own vileness, except by reference to something great with which we may compare it. It is in vain that we think of the little that is in us; we shall never be any the more humble, unless we compare it with the infinite perfections of God. It is thus that savages who inhabit

---

[1] E. Herman, *The Secret Garden of the Soul*, pp. 141–2.
[2] S. Teresa, *The Interior Castle*, Fourth Mansion, Chap. II., pp. 75–7.

forests are insensible to the wretchedness of their condition, until they come to know the manner of life of
civilised people, who dwell in towns in the midst of every
sort of accommodation; and so a poor villager will
never have any true idea of his poverty until he has seen
the mansions of the rich and the palaces of princes. We
may endure contempt from different motives:

    1. From a sense of the vanity of human esteem,
for in truth the honour and esteem of men are
nothing but vanity.

    2. From a motive of humility, because we deserve
every kind of disgrace.

    3. From a motive of fidelity, which constrains us
to render to God what belongs to Him, and to Him
alone belong honour and glory;

    4. From a motive of love and gratitude, inasmuch
as our Lord clothed Himself with ignominies, and
consecrated contempt and abjection in His adorable
Person." [1]

But the most important part of his task here is for the
director to lead the soul to perfect renunciation. S. John
of the Cross explains why this is so when he says: "The
state of divine union consists in the total transformation
of the will into the will of God, in such a way that every
movement of the will shall be always the movement of the
will of God only. This is the reason why in this state
two wills are said to be one—my will and God's will—
so that the will of God is also that of the soul. But if
the soul then cleaves to any imperfection, contrary to the
will of God, His will is not done, for the soul wills that
which God wills not. It is clear therefore that, if the
soul is to be united in love and will with God, every

[1] *Op. cit.*, pp. 286–7.

K

desire of the will must first of all be cast away, however
slight it may be; that is, we must not deliberately and
knowingly assent with the will to any imperfection, and
we must have such power over it, and such liberty, as to
reject every such desire the moment we are aware of it.
I say knowingly, for without deliberation and a clear
perception of what we are doing, or because it is not
wholly in our power, we may easily give way to imperfections and venial sins, and to those natural desires of
which I have just spoken. It is of such sins as these, not
so entirely voluntary, that it is written: ' A just man
shall fall seven times, and shall rise again.' But as to
those voluntary and perfectly deliberate desires, how
slight soever their object may be, any one of them, not
overcome, is sufficient to prevent this union. I am
speaking of the unmortified habit thereof, because
certain acts occasionally have not so much power, for
the habit of them is not settled; still, we must get rid of
them, for they, too, proceed from habitual imperfection.
Habits of voluntary imperfections, so far as they are
never perfectly overcome, hinder not only the divine
union, but our progress towards perfection. These
habitual imperfections are, for instance, much talking,
certain attachments, which we never resolve to break
through—such as to individuals, to a book or a cell, to a
particular food, to certain society, the satisfaction of
one's taste, science, news, and such things. Every one
of these imperfections, if the soul is attached and habituated to them, results in serious injuries to our growth and
progress in goodness. Yea, even if we fall daily into
many other imperfections greater than these, provided
they are not the result of the habitual indulgence of any
evil inclination, we should not be so much hindered
in our spiritual course as we are by this selfish attachment of the soul to particular objects; for while the soul

entertains it, it is useless to hope that we can ever attain to perfection, even though the object of our attachment be but of the slightest importance possible. Does it make any difference whether a bird be held by a slender thread or by a rope? While the bird is bound it cannot fly till the cord that holds it is broken. It is true that a slender thread is more easily broken, still, notwithstanding, if it is not broken the bird cannot fly. This is the state of a soul with particular attachments; it can never attain to the liberty of the divine union, whatever virtues it may possess. Desires and attachments affect the soul as the *remora* is said to affect a ship; that is but a little fish, yet when it clings to the vessel it effectually hinders its progress." [1]

However much the soul may work to attain this perfect surrender, it cannot succeed by its own unaided efforts. God must also participate by way of the purification of the Dark Night. And during this time of purgation the soul will need much encouragement if she is to persevere and place her whole trust in God.

Conclusion

We have thus traced the progress of the Christian soul from its introduction into the spiritual life up to the threshold of the Unitive Way. Not all souls follow exactly the same path, for each soul is different, and God distributes His gifts according to his good pleasure.

But still there are, as we have seen, certain ordinary stages by which the soul advances in the ways of perfection. Why is it that we do not advance more rapidly, and, alas! often either stand still, or even slip back? Is it not that we do not respond faithfully enough to the grace given us by God? For who could set bounds to the generosity of God were we always to respond to His

[1] *The Ascent of Mount Carmel*, pp. 46–8.

advances! God calls us all to be perfect, and in order
that we may be perfect, He gives us His own perfection.
And the reason why this perfection remains undeveloped
is our own lack of self-surrender and mortification.
" If any man will come after me, let him deny himself,
take up his cross, and follow me." [1]

[1] Matt. 16, 24.

APPENDIX

APPENDIX

HOW TO TEACH CHILDREN TO PRAY
By Walter de Lara Wilson

Before dealing with a child's prayer life, we must consider the foundation of character on which it must be built up. " Give me a child until he is seven, and then it does not matter who has him afterwards." Many may perhaps be inclined to challenge this statement when they think of cases where the child, well brought up for the first few years of life, yet suffers deeply in character from the evil influences of a later period. But the emphasis of the statement is really on the first few words. If we want a child to reach Edinburgh we may say that it is all important that he should be put in the right train. Of course, it is of vital importance that the train in which the child is put should be on lines running in the direction of Edinburgh, but in stating this we do not deny the fact that his ultimate arrival at his destination will depend on whether engine-drivers and signal-men and many other officials continue to do their duty. So the old Jesuit saying only emphasises in strong language the immense importance of the right direction of tendencies in early life.

In *Christian Experience and Psychological Processes*, Dr. Crichton Miller tells us that whereas once the thoughts of scientific people were fixed on physiology (the science of the body), now they are fixed on the science of the mind; and he suggests that our mistakes are certain to be many unless it is remembered all the time that there is yet another science, that of the spirit. We instinctively recognise the difference between an animal and a child. However affectionate or intelligent a dog may be, there is a mysterious and baffling lack in his nature; there is not that in him which is quite evidently present in the tiniest child, the something that responds at once to any suggestion or teaching about the unseen. "God breathed into man the breath of life and man became a living soul." [1] In man there is at the root or heart of his being a spark of the divine. It seems to be for this reason that the word heart is often used as synonymous with "spirit." "Thou shalt love the Lord thy God with all thy heart and with all thy mind." [2]

In the training of a child's character the end in view must always be that the child may "know God and enjoy Him for ever." A man of moral character does right actions, but a perfect man does right actions from the motive of pleasing God. In each case there is a choice at the back of the action, for man is not a machine; but in each case there may be one of two reasons for the choice; either a *self*-regarding or a *God*-regarding reason. If a child gives a penny to a beggar simply because it sees its mother do so, the action is not really the child's. It might equally well have been done by a monkey. But when the child really sees the lesson of the action and gives its penny knowing why it does so, then the action is part of itself. This means that in the early stages of will-training we should seek deliberately to make the action to be willed appear to the child not only possible, but desirable. For example, a child must learn to walk, *i.e.* he must perform certain actions over and over again until the nerves and muscles of the body act

[1] Gen. ii. 7.   [2] Matt. xxii. 37.

easily in connection with these movements he is making, and walking becomes a habit. For these first walking efforts obstacles are removed from in front of the child, while its mother stands a few yards off with arms outstretched to welcome him. The absence of obstacles makes the action of walking seem possible to the child and the hope of the mother's embrace makes the action desirable. So the child makes his first effort. In time he will have gained sufficient command of himself to surmount the obstacles and to do so in response to the idea of a remote, perhaps unseen spiritual good. Some day in a snowstorm he will walk miles down a country lane to visit an invalid because his Lord said: Inasmuch as ye did it unto one of these, ye did it unto me.[1]

So often the question is somewhat anxiously asked: " How soon do you think Peter and Susan ought to begin to say their prayers? " and the only true answer seems to be: " Never." It is so like the old story of the man asking the Irishman the way to Roscommon and getting the startling answer, " Well, now, if I was going to Roscommon I wouldn't be starting from here at all." So much religious teaching and our own efforts in the spiritual life fail because we start from the wrong place.

Our starting-point lies surely in the realisation that, since children have God's life and Spirit within them, we do not have to begin to teach them about God as if we were introducing some strange element into their lives. Our part is rather to be ready to help and not hinder the right development of that sense of the divine which they instinctively possess, so that " all things belonging to the Spirit may live and grow in them."

No mother ever asks with desperate anxiety, " How shall I begin to teach my child to talk, and how soon

[1] Matt. xxv. 40.

ought I to begin?" She knows that in the life of every normal healthy child this development will come quite simply and naturally. Of course if the child never hears anyone talking, if there is no talk going on around him and no words are said to him, he will not produce words himself, but only vague sounds of demand, or complaint or pleasure, as a deaf child might. But if he hears words continually, and with them gradually associates his dawning discrimination of people and things, he will begin to use them himself, and by experiment find out more and more of their real use and meaning.

If there is not the stimulus of any definite recognition of God in the child's environment, and little or no apparent reference by those around him to spiritual realities, he will remain inarticulate and retarded, if not altogether thwarted, in this development. What we have to consider most is how we can create and sustain around the child that spiritual condition to which his growing capacity can make response.

It is not what we teach, but what we believe that is going to influence the child's whole life. The danger of truisms like this is that we get so used to hearing them that we forget that they are true. The more we know of little children the more we become aware of how much they absorb the influences with which they are surrounded. It is, then, on this indirect teaching more than on any direct teaching by word that a great deal, if not everything, will depend in the child's religious education. The supreme knowledge that we want children to receive is that God is love, but they must learn about this first of all by living in an atmosphere pervaded by this fundamental truth. If they live in an atmosphere where material and selfish interests prevail, and where success and " a good time " are the chief objects in life, they will never be able to feel that

Christian teaching applies to their everyday life. If they are associating the idea of parental control with a sense of repression, or with a capricious kind of affection and lack of sympathy and understanding, or with a continual fear of punishment, what sort of ideas will they form of the Fatherhood of God? How many boys and girls give up going to Communion after a failure to wrestle with temptations against purity or some other sin because they have had implanted in them at an early stage the idea that " God doesn't love you when you're naughty? "

We need not labour this point; but a good deal of our difficulty, it seems, in dealing with children is to get rid of these early wrong impressions which, whether consciously or unconsciously, cloud their minds and hide God's infinite love for them. It is almost impossible to teach a child to pray in any real sense to a being who has been associated in their minds with punishment and disapproval and cold severity, instead of with that glowing love which heals while it hurts.

It is a great hindrance in teaching set forms of prayer to children to expect them to use the second person singular. The " Thee " and the " Thou " and the verbs accompanying them sound strange and forced to a little child. It is much easier to say, " Thank you, dear Jesus," than to say, " I thank Thee, Lord." Another point is that we who are their teachers must pray *with the children*, rather than say prayers in their hearing— always of course excepting the times of liturgical and other formal worship. Those things do not come within the scope of this note.

The idea of waiting upon God, which older people so often find so difficult to recapture, is not unnatural to a child. Always try to get stillness first, and, as it were, a time of " listening to God " before beginning any actual prayers. It also seems important to add, that children should be taught from the earliest that prayer is not *asking* all the time; that adoration or worship is the chief part of prayer, and that next to this comes thanksgiving.

It is impossible to *make* children pray. Again, a heavy forced solemnity has obviously nothing to do with reverence, and drives from religion those qualities of joy and freshness which should be at the heart of it. An unnatural forced stillness at prayer time thwarts and hinders the inborn capacity for worship which is to be found in children. It is an entirely wrong idea to divide life into two departments of secular and sacred. We want the holy things to be in real relation to everyday life. In this connection children should be encouraged to go quite naturally into church as they pass, for a moment's stillness and worship. This is particularly valuable in parishes where poor homes or slums make any attempt at proper prayer in their own homes next to impossible.

" Children's Corners " are not suitable perhaps in all parishes, but in slum parishes a set place for their own books and objects of devotion and pictures which suggest worship to the child mind is a great help in encouraging them to use the church at times other than those of Mass and Catechism.

Confession must never be forced on a child, and, in this connection, it is easier for a child to say " Forgive me, dear Jesus, for hurting you," than to say, " Forgive me for being naughty." There is a delightful book, edited by Margaret Cropper, called *Elizabeth June*, in which is to be found the following conversation. In the book the story is told of the day when Elizabeth, aged three, in a rage at lunch, flung her spoons and plate on the floor. This is the conversation between herself and her mother at prayer-time that evening. The incident of the spoons came up, and the mother says: " Well, we just say sorry, 'cos He knows you were."

> E. " Did I throw those spoons at Jesus? "
>
> M. (rather afraid at making too heavy an impression and yet unable to deny). " Yes, it was rather like that, wasn't it? Only you didn't think of that when you did it."
>
> E. " No, but did it hurt Him—was it putting Him on the Cross? "
>
> M. " Yes, but it stopped hurting the minute you were sorry."
>
> E. (relieved) " So it's all right now. He's not on the Cross now? "
>
> M. " Oh no, only so happy, because you're sorry and love Him."

On such a basis sacramental Confession and its value and use are easily taught.

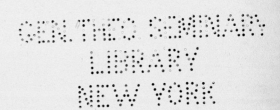

LIST OF WORKS CITED

Baker, A., O.S.B., *The Inner Life of Dame Gertrude More*. Burns, Oates, and Washbourne, London, 1920.

Bérulle, Card. de, *La Direction Spirituelle*. Desclée, 1926; *Œuvres Complètes*, Migne, 1856.

Besse, L. de, O.F.M., *The Science of Prayer*. Burns, Oates, and Washbourne, London, 1925.

Bremond, H., *Histoire Littéraire du Sentiment Religieux en France*, Toms. ii. and iii. Blond et Gay, Paris, 1914. English translation of Vol. II., *A Literary History of Religious Thought in France*. S.P.C.K., London, 1930.

Brétonvilliers, A. de, *L'Esprit d'un Directeur des Âmes*.

Butler, Cuthbert, O.S.B., *Ways of Christian Life*. Sheed and Ward, London, 1932; *Western Mysticism*, 2nd Ed. Constable & Co., London, 1926.

Chautard, J. B., O.C.R., *L'Âme de Tout Apostolat*. Téqui, Paris, 1930.

Crichton-Miller, *Christian Experience and Psychological Processes*.

De Bernières-Louvigny, Treasurer of France, *Le Chrétien Intérieur, ou la Conformité Intérieure que doivent avoir les Chrétiens avec Jésus Christ, par un Solitaire*, 12th Ed., English translation, *The Interior Christian*, esp. Book VII., on Prayer. 1684.

Desurmont, *La Charité Sacerdotale*. Téqui, Paris, 1925.

Faber, F. W., *Growth in Holiness*. Burns, Oates, and Washbourne London.

Frost, B., O.S.B., *The Art of Mental Prayer* (for S. Pedro de Alcántara, S. Alphonsus, V. John of Jesus Mary). Philip Allan, London, 1931.

Gay, Mgr., *Lettres de Direction Spirituelle*. Oudin, Paris, 1912.

Grou, J., S.J., *A Manual for Interior Souls*. Burns, Oates, and Washbourne, London, 1927.

Herman, E., *The Secret Garden of the Soul*. J. Clarke, London, 1924.

Hilton, Walter, *The Scale of Perfection*. Art and Book Co., London, 1908.

Hollings, *One Born of the Spirit*. Masters.

Hooker, Richard, *Ecclesiastical Polity*.

Joly, H., *The Psychology of the Saints*. Duckworth, London, 1902.

Kempis, S. Thomas à, *The Imitation of Christ*. Rivingtons, London, 1888.

Kirk, K. E., *The Vision of God*. Longmans, 1931.

Lallemant, L., S.J., *Spiritual Teaching*. Burns, Oates, and Washbourne, London, 1908.

Leonard, J. C. M., *S. Vincent de Paul and Mental Prayer*. Burns, Oates, and Washbourne, London, 1925.

Libermann, Ven. P., *Lettres Spirituelles*. Poussielque Fs., Paris ; *Spiritual Writings*.

Liddon, H. P., *Some Elements of Religion*. Rivingtons, London, 1873.

Longridge, W. H., S.S.J.E., *Retreats for Priests*. Mowbrays, London, 1930.

McHugh and Callan, *Moral Theology*. Herder, New York.

Maritain, J., *De la Vie d'Oraison*. A l'Art Catholique, Paris, 1924.

Marmion, C., O.S.B., *La Christ dan ses Mystères*. Lethielleux, Paris, 1926.

Olier, J.-J., *Oeuvres Complètes*. Migne, 1856.

Poulain, A., S.J., *The Prayer of Simplicity*. Catholic Truth Society.

Pourrat, P., *Christian Spirituality*, Vol. III. (for Luis de Granada). Burns, Oates, and Washbourne, London.

Ravignan, *Spiritual Conferences*. Burns, Oates, and Washbourne, London, 1903.

S. Bernard, *Sermon for Ascension*. Pasimblum, Venice, 1750.

S. Chrysostom, *Homily on Genesis ; Homily on Prayer*.

S. Francis de Sales, *Introduction à la Vie Dévote*. Gabalda, 1928; *Spiritual Conferences*. Burns, Oates, and Washbourne, London, 1909; *A Treatise on the Love of God*. Keating and Brown, London, 1836.

S. John of the Cross, *The Living Flame of Love*. T. Baker, London, 1912; *The Dark Night of the Soul*. T. Baker, London, 1908; *The Ascent of Mount Carmel*. T. Baker, London, 1906.

S. Teresa, *The Way of Perfection*. T. Baker, London, 1911; *The Interior Castle*. T. Baker, London, 1906.

Saudreau, A., *The Degrees of the Spiritual Life*. Burns, Oates, and Washbourne, London, 1907.

Sharpe, *Perfection and the Only Alternative*. Simpkins Marshall.

Surin, J.-J., S.J., *A Spiritual Catechism*.

Tanquerey, A., *Précis de Théologie Ascétique et Mystique*. Desclée, 1928.

Thompson, E. H., *Life of M. Olier*.

Tissot, *The Interior Life*. Burns, Oates, and Washbourne, London, 1913.

Van Acken, *A Handbook for Sisters*. Herder, 1931.

Vonier, A., O.S.B., *The Human Soul*. Herder, 1913.

Wilberforce, S., *Ordination Addresses*.

Williamson, *The Triumph of Love*. Kegan Paul, London, 1923.

PRINTED IN GREAT BRITAIN BY RICHARD CLAY & SONS, LIMITED, BUNGAY, SUFFOLK.

DATE DUE